JAMES MARTIN

Riada Macmillan.

it's you minister

JAMES MARTIN

Copyright © 1990 by James Martin

First edition published 1990 by Chapter House Ltd
26 Bothwell Street, Glasgow G2 6PA.

ISBN 0 948643 07 2

Production and Printing in England by
NUPRINT LIMITED
30b Station Road, Harpenden, Herts AL5 4SE.

contents

dedication

This book is dedicated to
Bill McColl
and all those others in various
churches who have been my true
and constant friends.

introduction

it's you, minister

For anyone genuinely called to the Christian ministry—and who would take it on unless they felt a strong sense of vocation?—there is always much more on the plus than on the minus side, invariably much more happiness than misery.

At the same time, by the very nature of his calling, the minister is particularly and peculiarly vulnerable to criticism that is unfair and to hurt that is undeserved. He often may get a fair number (some would say *unfair* number) of slaps in the face and even kicks in the teeth. This is no doubt due to the fact that in the performance of his job he is much involved with people; and human nature can be such a perverse thing at times.

There is an old ministerial story which goes like this. "Mum," called out little Susan, standing by the window, "Here's the minister walking down our street."

"What an inconvenient time for him to choose to call, with me in the middle of washing the floor," said mother. Hurriedly taking off her apron and drying her hands, she got to the window just in time to see the minister pass her gate and make his way further down the street. "Would you believe it? He walks past my very gate and won't even take time to come in and say hello!"

That story is allegedly apocryphal but sometimes I wonder. It could so easily have been an actual occurrence. I can tell you, at any rate, that one minister joke that is frequently told actually happened to me. Once, during an afternoon's visitation, my knock upon a certain door was answered by a little girl who, on seeing me, immediately rushed back inside, shouting, "Mum, there's a man at the door." Her cry brought her mother to the door and, when she caught sight of me, she turned to her daughter and said, "That's not a man! That's the minister."

For a long time—although the practice is less universal now than it once was—the minister has worn his collar back to front as a kind of badge of office. This clerical collar is colloquially—and, I hope, affectionately—known as 'the dog collar'. That is why at one stage I intended to give this book the title 'The Collar and the Chain'. Dog collars sometimes have chains attached to them for restraining and restrictive purposes. The minister for his part is 'chained' to his job and at times this may prove restrictive to the point of considerable frustration.

But there is a great deal more to it than that.

This book is a gathering together of incidents and people remembered from my ministry, spent partly in a small country town in Ayrshire and mainly in a large city parish in Glasgow. They reflect something of the joys and the sorrows, the irritations and the encouragements, the disappointments and the satisfactions that are common to all ministers and to all congregations.

chapter one

giving the minister his place

"We simply won't allow it," John Cochrane was saying to me across his desk, the managing director's, in Hood Morton's lace factory in Newmilns. I was sitting on the other side of the desk that day because John Cochrane was also the Preses (that is, chairman) of the management committee of Newmilns West Church and I was the minister.

As he spoke, my thoughts winged back to the night nearly a year ago when I had been ordained and inducted to the pastoral charge of Newmilns West; and I said to myself, "The honeymoon period is over right enough".

One of the speakers at the social evening held to welcome me following my induction had remarked, whimsically, but at the same time, as I was now aware, more than a little seriously, "Remember that ministers tend to repeat an established pattern—first year, idolised; second year, criticised; third year, scandalised", and now I had come face to face with some of the promised criticism.

The service of ordination and induction had been a deeply moving experience for me. The ministers and elders who constituted the Presbytery sat at the front of the church with the congregation filling the rest of the downstairs area and spilling over into the gallery in large numbers. I did not remember very much of the service but I recalled vividly the questions that were put to me, as to all standing in a similar situation, particularly question number six, "Are not zeal for the glory of God, love to the Lord Jesus Christ, and a desire for the salvation of men, so far as you know your own heart, your great motives and chief inducements to enter into the office of the holy ministry?" How humbled and uplifted I had felt then at one and the same time; and how eager to get on with the work to which I was so sure that God had called me. And here I was now, nearly a year later, involved in another of the situations that were making it plain to me that the minister's job was not all smooth sailing.

A remark made at the welcome social by one of the elders came back to me, "We like to get our ministers young and give them a training. But I warn you that we pride ourselves on calling a spade a spade". I did not realise at the time that this really meant, "We like to mould young ministers into our ways"—but I knew it now. I knew also that they were not always content to call a spade a spade but sometimes to refer to it as a blooming shovel.

And here I was—young and still very raw— engaged in a 'head to head' with a man who was not only a leading light in my church but also a leading light in the industrial life of the town.

Little though I could have imagined it at the time, such a confrontation had been more or less certain from the time I had started up a weeknight Youth Club and a Sunday night Youth Fellowship, neither of which activities had previously been known in Newmilns West Church. This involved, of course, additional usage of the church halls, and the church officer was none too thrilled by the extra work and time consequently demanded of him (although he later became one of my best friends and staunchest allies).

Our official finishing hour was 9.30 p.m. but by the time we cleared away and tidied up it was often much nearer ten o'clock before the premises could be locked up. The church officer insisted on locking up in person. And, although he lived beside the church, the additional chore made him a bit resentful and eventually he wrote a letter of complaint to the church's management committee. This was the body, elected from members of the congregation, who administered the material side of affairs in the church, including property.

The result was that on this particular morning the postman had delivered to me—to my utter surprise—a letter from the Clerk to the managers which informed me of their displeasure at the time keeping of these youth organisations. It went on to order (sic!) me to ensure that the halls were cleared by 9.30 p.m. or they would be forced to withdraw from me permission to use them for these purposes.

Young and inexperienced as I was, I nevertheless was fully aware that the managers did not in fact have the power to do what they were threatening to do. Even under the Newmilns West Church style of constitution, the minister, as in all Church of Scotland congregations, had absolute authority regarding the use of any of the church premises for youth activities such as we were having.

I immediately telephoned Mr. Cochrane requesting an interview, and here I was sitting facing him across his managerial desk. I had taken the precaution of also telephoning the Presbytery Clerk before coming to see John Cochrane in order to have his official confirmation of what I already knew to be my rights and authority. I was unwilling, however, to provoke any unpleasantness by adopting a belligerent attitude. I was, in any case, more than a little in awe of this much older man, widely experienced and very successful in the business world.

"I'm greatly concerned and disappointed," I said, "about the letter I received this morning from the management committee."

"Well," was his reply, "we can't have you occupying the halls to all hours. We simply won't allow it. The managers have decided that 9.30 p.m. is absolutely the latest you can be permitted in the halls. If that time is not suitable for your meetings, I am afraid you will just have to discontinue them altogether."

I realised that I would, after all, have to play my trump card and at once. "Mr. Cochrane," I said, "the managers can't do that. In the Church of Scotland the minister has complete authority over the use of the premises for religious purposes. I could go on until midnight with my youth groups if I chose, with or without the approval of the managers."

"You seem to be forgetting, Mr. Martin," was his rejoinder, "that we are a former United Presbyterian congregation. As such we have our own constitution and are not bound by the same church laws as most other congregations."

He spoke with great conviction and I was very glad that I had taken the trouble to verify with the Presbytery Clerk what the correct position was.

"No, no, Mr. Cochrane," I insisted, "That is not quite so. I have consulted with the Presbytery Clerk and he affirms that, no matter what type of constitution any individual congregation may have, it is always the case that the minister has absolute authority over the use of church premises for religious purposes."

Mr. Cochrane was considerably less impressed than I had confidently expected him to be.

"I am sure that does not apply where we are concerned." And then came a hammer blow to my youthful pride. "In any case, Mr. Martin, you must remember that ministers are birds of passage but church officers are hard to come by."

My heart sank. To think that I had believed so uncritically all the things that had been said at my welcome social about how pleased they were to get me and how talented I was and what great things they were expecting with me at the helm. But I stuck to my guns—rather tremblingly, if the truth be told.

"I'm going to carry on with my youth groups despite what you say," I said. "Because I know that

you have no real power to stop me. But I will under-
take to lock up the premises myself and so save the
church officer being disturbed."

And that is how the matter was left.

A week or two later, just to ram home the
point to my own satisfaction, three of the boys and I
stayed behind one Club night after the others had
dispersed and played table-tennis until two o'clock in
the morning.

In the cold light of the following day, I recognised this for the rather foolish act of bravado it
undoubtedly was and I never repeated it.

How much I enjoyed it all the same! In fact, it
was one of the most enjoyable sessions of table-tennis
I ever remember.

chapter two

the watchnight service

"I don't want to throw cold water on it but I very much doubt if it will be a success."

It was December 1944 and the speaker was John Miller, session clerk of Newarthill Parish Church. I was acting as locum tenens there at the end of my college course in the absence of the minister who was serving as an army chaplain. With the end of the year approaching, I had suggested that we hold a watchnight service in the church to bring in the New Year.

John Miller and I had a very happy relationship. He seemed to like my youthful enthusiasm and I greatly valued his kindly wisdom.

"I wouldn't like you to get a big disappointment," he continued, "and I'm afraid that with the blackout and one thing and another, people just won't want to be out of their homes so late at night."

He could see plainly, however, that I was keen to go ahead and he did not want to stand in my way. The kirk session approved and the watchnight service was announced.

It could scarcely have been more successful. The church was packed, the atmosphere was terrific and everyone counted the occasion an outstanding success.

Exactly two years later it almost seemed to me

15

that I had been caught up in some kind of time-warp. Deja vu was certainly an appropriate term.

"I don't want to be a wet blanket but I don't think it will work here."

Again it was my session clerk who was speaking, the words were much similar and once more the subject at issue was my proposal to hold a watchnight service in the church on New Year's Eve. But the church was Newmilns West of which I was the still quite new minister and the session clerk was Ernest Ling.

"I wouldn't like you to suffer disappointment," he continued, "but I feel sure the people just won't turn out. They will prefer to see in the New Year in their own homes as they have always done."

I knew better, of course. My Newarthill experience had shown that I was on sure ground. Two highly successful watchnight services there assured me that they were bound to be popular in Newmilns, too. And so I pressed ahead. The kirk session gave their consent, although a number of elders indicated that they themselves would be following their usual practice of bringing in the New Year in their own homes. This was a disappointment to me as I wanted the church to be as crowded as it could possibly be; but, then, there were plenty of other people to fill the pews.

This time the session clerk was right and I was wrong. What a flop the service turned out to be! The congregation numbered twelve, including myself and I can still feel the disappointment these many years after.

Eight years later I found myself part of a very similar scenario; I was pestering the kirk session at

High Carntyne to let me have a Christmas Eve watchnight service.

I had never again attempted a New Year's Eve
watchnight service in Newmilns and, since our neigh-
bour Church of Loudoun Old always held a Christmas
Eve watchnight service which served the whole town,
I had never had such a service in Newmilns West
either. But now that I had moved to High Carntyne I
was keen to try my own Christmas Eve service.

This was something that High Carntyne had
never had before and the initial reaction of the kirk
session was adverse. "It won't work. The people won't
come. You'll just get a terrible disappointment."

"How about having a Hogmanay service
instead?" one elder suggested. But, I had quite

enough of that, thank you; and in any case I felt strongly that a watchnight service for Christmas Eve was something that ought to be made available.

The kirk session—bless them—were anxious to humour the new minister in what was to be his first Christmas with them, and there was never any real doubt but that they would eventually give the go-ahead. They were, however, genuinely fearful that the service would be ill-attended and that I would be hurt. Without exception they were convinced the experiment would be a disaster and many of them went out of their way to prepare me for it and so soften the impact when it came.

"Don't expect too much. After all, we've never had anything like this before."

"Don't build up your hopes too high. This is something that will likely take a year or two to catch on."

"You're not to take it personally if hardly anyone turns up. It's such a new thing for us."

Our church officer Johnny Kincaid, a minister's man if ever there was one—was particularly anxious to protect me as much as he could from the disappointment he felt was inevitable.

"Our people don't take easily to new ideas. and we had a Hogmanay watchnight service once and the church was almost empty."

"I had one the very same in Newmilns," I said. "But I'm hoping a Christmas Eve midnight service will be different."

"No, no," replied Johnny, "they'll just no' come oot sae late at night. Just don't expect much and you'll no' be disappointed. But *I'll* be here anyway."

Came the night and by this time I was full of foreboding, pretty much reconciled to a repeat of my

Newmilns fiasco. The service was to begin at 11.30 p.m. and Johnny Kincaid had decided to pretend optimism and open the church at 11 o'clock. But before that hour was reached, he observed a group of people gathered on the street outside the church gates.

"I was sure," he told me later, "that they had come to the wrong church. I said to them, 'You'll be looking for the Catholic church and their midnight mass. Well, it's down the road there', and they said, 'We're doing nothing of the kind. We're here to attend Mr. Martin's service'."

"You know," he went on, "you could have knocked me down with a feather. I never expected any more than half a dozen altogether."

You could have knocked me down with the same feather long before half past eleven. Well before that time the church was packed to capacity. People were sitting everywhere, even on the pulpit steps, and standing in every available space. When I began the

service, there were fully a thousand in the church and a hundred or more standing outside.

For me certainly—and for many others, too, I think—there was a sound of angels in the air that Christmas Eve.

chapter three

the locum's lot is a happy one

Sometimes I have thought to myself that it could have been almost perfect if I had been able to be a locum tenens all my working life.

What made some later experiences so traumatic, such as my confrontation with the Preses in Newmilns West Church, was that I had been considerably spoiled during the year and a half I spent at Newarthill as locum tenens in the village church. With the minister away on army chaplaincy service, I was invited to serve there as locum, when I finished my divinity training course.

I received payment of £200 per annum. As I look back on it, I realise that this was by no means overpayment, considering that I was doing all the ministerial work except for the tasks that required an ordained person, namely, marriages, baptisms and communions. But I loved it—not least, I think, because the Newarthill people seemed to love me.

That is, I can assure you, the usual good fortune of the assistant minister and the locum tenens. The minister, poor soul, is the one with whom 'the buck stops.' He gets the blame for everything that may happen to go wrong, even if he has had nothing at all to do with the fact that it went wrong. An irate mother once illustrated this point very vividly to me in my

High Carntyne days when she began to berate me
quite vehemently on account of some remark that had
been made to her small son at Sunday School. As soon
as I could manage to get a word in, I protested as
mildly as I was able, "I am very sorry that you have
been upset, but why are you blaming me? It wasn't
my doing and, as a matter of fact, I didn't even know
about it until this very moment when you told me."

"Of course I'm blaming you!" she retorted.
"Everything that happens in the church is your
responsibility."

The assistant and the locum, on the other
hand, have to shoulder none of that kind of blame.
They are not responsible for policy or practice; no
fingers are pointed at them if somewhere things
should chance to go awry. It can be a great life being a
locum or an assistant; and, if you should be young in
years as I was in Newarthill, it can be simply marvellous.

I was locum tenens at Newarthill for eighteen
months—probably just about the ideal length of time.
It was long enough to accomplish what, I hope, was
something worthwhile; but not long enough for the
congregation to get utterly tired of me. Nearly everything I put my hand to seemed to be touched with
success.

Attendances at the Sunday services increased
and maintained their increased level. I would like to
believe that this was a sign of consistently outstanding preaching on my part—and no doubt that is what
I believed at the time. But my memory of those days is
too good to allow me such a misapprehension—and
my memory is backed up by the survival of some of
my sermon manuscripts of that period. The fact is that
some of the sermons I preached were pretty awful;

others, I think and hope, were not too bad. The marvellous thing is—at the time very gratifying to me and now, in retrospect, extremely humbling—that the congregation were so responsive, turning out faithfully Sunday after Sunday and giving the impression both of enjoying what I had to say and of deriving benefit from it.

The Bible Class was also a roaring success, both in numbers and in enthusiasm; and it was tremendous encouragement and help to me in many ways. I often wonder if I did anything very much for them, but its members undoubtedly did a very great deal for me.

Newarthill was great fun and I learned many things there that were of immense help in my future ministry. It did have disadvantages, however, so far as that future ministry was concerned. It did not prepare me in any real measure for the disappointments and discouragements that are inevitably part of the scene of every parish ministry. Nor for the fact that what may work like a dream in one congregation may be more like a nightmare in another—like the New Year's Eve watchnight service, for example.

Of course, to be perfectly honest, not everything I attempted even in Newarthill was a resounding success. The elders' service was one experiment that was anything but.

I thought it would be a good idea for the elders (all men in those days) to carry through an entire church service. They agreed and so such a service was planned. I arranged for elders to read the scripture lessons, elders to lead prayers, elders to do the stewarding, elders to sing, elders to...and I persuaded George Park to preach the sermon.

George was a miner who had had the minimum of formal schooling but whose Christian faith was a vibrant, living reality; and I thought it would be a marvellous witness to the Gospel just to have him in the pulpit to deliver a few simple words about what Jesus Christ meant to him.

George had never done any public speaking before and was naturally apprehensive when I put the proposition to him. But I managed to get him to agree to do it and between us a simple short address was prepared. I spent hours going over it with him time after time after time. He was anxious to have it learned off by heart so that he would not need to refer to his script.

By the day of the service he was word perfect. It was to be an evening service and in the afternoon we had a rehearsal of sorts in the church—with all the participants. It went very well and I was full of very pleasant anticipation.

For the service itself I occupied the pulpit with George beside me and introduced the items of the service and the various individuals responsible for them. In due course we came to the sermon. I made my brief introduction of George and sat down. George stood up and we all waited for him to begin. But no words came. Still we waited and still he did not speak. Then he turned to me and in agonised tones he whispered, "I can't do it. I'm sorry but I can't do it."

I did what I could to salvage the service. I got to my feet and, explaining that George did not feel well enough to deliver the address himself, I tried to give the gist of what he was to have said. But it was a poor, poor substitute for what was to have been. That elders' service finished up a painful experience for all concerned—and, of course, for George most of all. To this day I have regrets that my misjudgement led to such pain for him.

But some good came of it so far as I was concerned. From that time on I have been more concerned, as Christians of course always should be, to try to put myself in the other person's place.

chapter four

the assistant

The minister's assistant (the 'helper' as he used to be called in days gone by) was and is a breed apart. Some cynic once described the minister's assistant as 'the lowest form of animal life known to man'; but I have no doubt that remark was never meant to be taken seriously.

I, for my part at any rate, look back with much pleasure and considerable gratitude on the assistants I had in High Carntyne. Over the years I had quite a number of them—and that is without including my wife, the 'unpaid assistant' whom I had—thank God—all the time. Nowadays it is the regular thing for the minister's wife to be engaged in paid employment outside the church; but when I entered the ministry, for the minister's wife to 'go out to work' was rare and in most congregations would have been met with considerable disapproval.

My wife, then, like most of her manse contemporaries, did not have a job outside of the manse and the church; and she gave a lot of her time and energy to assisting the work I was seeking to do. For this she was unpaid, of course, and at times perhaps unappreciated. This was too often the lot of manse wives who gave much service in various ways to their husbands' churches.

Of them, too, there is a cynical and apocryphal story told, perhaps in illustration of this point. A certain minister and his wife had been on holiday abroad and a social function was held to welcome them back. The senior elder offered a prayer in the following terms: "We thank Thee, O God, that Thou hast brought our minister safely back to us—and his wife, too, for Thou, Lord, preservest man and beast."

It is beyond doubt that the minister's wife has often been a (willing) beast of burden in the life of the congregation and I am certainly grateful for the congregational burdens my wife took on her shoulders. But it is of my officially appointed assistants that this chapter set out to speak. It can be a tremendous boon to a minister to have a good assistant and mine were mostly good, some of them very good.

And when there is a real rapport between the minister and his assistant, as was the case much more than once in my experience, what a bonus that is for the minister, and perhaps for the assistant as well. Then the benefit derived is to be measured not only in terms of services conducted, sick visits made and that sort of thing. The chief benefit, as I found it, is to have a kindred mind and a sympathetic heart with whom to share things—plans, hopes, disappointments, annoyances.

It was inevitable, I suppose, that some of my assistants were more in the nature of 'soul-mates' to me than others were. But all were real 'helpers' in their own way and all of them I count as friends.

A number of them were mature students, most of whom had given up very good positions in industry or commerce in order to train for the ministry. Contrary to the cynical view sometimes expressed, not one of my assistants, whether younger or older, struck

me as being in it just for a job. For all of them it was a
calling. And of them I have many happy memories—
and not a few funny ones, too. Let me share with you
some of these.

To preserve their anonymity which I think is
only fair, I will refer to them simply as assistant one,
assistant two and so on, and this will have no chrono-
logical significance.

Perhaps my most vivid memory of Assistant
One is of the hilarious slips of the tongue he sometimes made. One Sunday morning, for instance, the
Gospel reading was from the Passion narrative. It was
hard for me to keep a straight face in the pulpit, never
mind preserve a dignified mien, when I heard him
declaim in sonorous tones: "And there were also two
other, *male factors*, crucified with him."

I did not quite succeed in keeping a straight
face on another occasion but managed, I think, to save
the day by developing a sudden cough which
required me to bury my face in my handkerchief. In
any event, I was not occupying the pulpit. I liked
every now and again to let my assistant have free
reign at the evening service. He would conduct the
whole service while I sat in the congregation. One
evening, the week before our quarterly communion
services, as he was reading our intimations I had
given him, we heard him announce in a voice that
brooked no argument, "Next Sunday the Sacrament of
the Lord's Supper will be dispensed *with* in this
church."

Assistant Two was sent by me one day to call
on an elderly widower who was housebound and
shared his house with his married daughter and her
husband. When he arrived, it was the old man who
answered his knock and, as he escorted him in, he

said, "The doctor has ordered my daughter to bed. Would you like to see her?" So Assistant Two duly followed his host into the room where the daughter lay abed. Approaching her, he said, "Well, now, what have you been doing to get yourself into this condition?" When he discovered that the lady was in an advanced stage of pregnancy and had been ordered to get some bed-rest, he felt that his opening words could have been better chosen—and fled the house as quickly as he could.

Assistant Three and I shared many exploits. One which he is always more ready to recount than I am took place in Glasgow's Buchanan Street. I had just obtained a new car—a shining Morris Minor—and proudly took Assistant Three with me for its 'baptismal' run. Having an errand to attend to in Glasgow, I parked the car in Buchanan Street and off we went together to see to whatever it was I had on hand. On returning to the car and inserting the key in the lock, I was horrified to find the door already unlocked. I knew that I had locked the car when we left it and my heart sank at the thought of some criminal illegally entering my brand new car, no doubt with the intention to make off with it. Thank goodness we had come back when we did. Another five minutes might well have meant disaster.

However no damage seemed to have been done, which was a great relief. "I think," said Assistant Three, "that you ought to report this attempted theft to the police."

"I suppose I should," I agreed. "It will at least alert them to the fact that there is a car thief operating in this area. We'll just drive round to the police station now and tell them."

So we slid into our seats, I inserted the ignition key and it wouldn't turn. I tried again and still it wouldn't turn. Assistant Three tried with no more success.

"Whoever it was," I cried, "has done some damage in trying to start the car illegally and now it won't start. That is probably why it's still here and not stolen."

My heart was in my boots and I was in the depths of despair. Then suddenly my emotions changed first to consternation and then to embarrassment. My eye caught sight of the milometer and I saw that it registered more than 200 miles. It was not my car!

It, too, was a new Morris Minor and it was the same colour; but it was someone else's car.

"This is not my car!" I yelled. "Let's get out of here fast before *we're* suspected of car stealing."

Out we tumbled, and there was my own car two spaces further up the street. It was a very red-faced minister and an assistant almost helpless with laughter who got into the right vehicle in double-quick time and drove away as speedily as possible from the locus delicti.

Usually I tried not to delegate any visits to the assistant that were likely to prove difficult or tricky but to attend to all such myself. There were occasions, however, when either the difficulty could not be foreseen or the difficulty was one in which the assistant was personally involved. One such visit was on the list when I had Assistant Four.

He had paid a run-of-the-mill visit to a certain lady who was temporarily housebound and they had got themselves involved in a bit of an argument. The upshot was that the lady in question—a notoriously

difficult character, I may say—felt mortally offended and said to my assistant when he took his leave, "I don't think much of you as a minister, I am afraid. I don't want any more ministerial visits from you."

Assistant Four duly reported all this to me at the weekly conference we had together and when the said lady's turn came round for another visit, I said, "I'd better make that visit this time."

"Please let me do it," pleaded Assistant Four. "I would like to try and make things right between her and me."

I rather feared, knowing the lady only too well, that he might be in for a stormy session but, since he was clearly set on it, I eventually gave in and let him have his way.

And in due course he found himself outside her door. He rang the bell and herself appeared.

"Before I let you in," she thundered, "tell me whether you have come to my door as a minister or as a gentleman?"

I am still trying to work that one out but there was no such mystery about another experience which I shared with Assistant Four.

I had recently purchased a new car from a dealer in the city. And one night I was driving in very heavy rain when—to my surprise, to my fright and to my danger—my windscreen wiper simply detached itself and vanished into the darkness. It was, I can tell you, a difficult and somewhat hazardous journey home.

The following day I took my car, still only a few weeks old, back to the garage from which it had been purchased. Assistant Four went with me, as he was interested to see the garage and what it had to offer. I was attended to by a young salesman whose attitude from the outset was supercilious, to say the least. We rather suspected that he was interested only in sales that might be made and not in sales that had already been made.

"Well, sir," he said, "what can I do for you?"—an unremarkable and certainly not hostile greeting.

"I bought a new car here about three weeks ago," I replied, and I could see his eyes begin to glaze over already with the recognition that here before him was not a fresh sale potential but in all probability a complaint of sorts. I pressed on with my tale of woe, "I was driving along the Motherwell to Bellshill road last night in pouring rain when all of a sudden the windscreen wiper blade on the driver's side blew away."

"What had you been doing with the wiper, sir?"

"I hadn't touched it."

"I don't mean at that precise moment, sir, but I presume you had been working with it in some way previously."

"No, I had never touched it in any way."

"I assure you, sir, that it would be impossible for the wiper blade to detach itself in the way you have described unless it had previously been tampered with."

"I assure *you* that never at any time during the three weeks I have owned the car did I do anything to that windscreen wiper and I am here to have you replace the loss I have sustained."

"I am afraid, sir," the maddeningly suave voice continued, "that we can not accept responsibility for your loss. I know for a fact that what you describe could not have happened if the wiper had not been interfered with."

Assistant Four's temper in those days of his youth had a much lower boiling point than it has now and I had been aware of the temperature rising within him as my conversation with the salesman proceeded. With this last remark he boiled over.

"Are you daring to suggest that my friend is telling lies?" he asked.

Slightly taken aback by the unmistakable menace in Assistant Four's tone, the salesman nonetheless persisted in his chosen attitude.

"I'm simply saying that his windscreen wiper could not have flown off if it had not been tampered with in some way."

Assistant Four could take no more. He was actually white with anger.

"What you're saying is offensive and insulting. My friend here, being a gentleman as well as a minister, won't take you up on it. But I will. It's obviously no good talking to you but I'd like you to step round the back of the premises so that I can let you know what I really think of you."

Oh, dear. The prospect of a punch-up on my behalf and in a semi-public place at that did not fill me with delight. Fortunately for all concerned the salesman proved that he had a measure of discretion, if not much courtesy, and he hastened, somewhat grudgingly, to arrange for my windscreen wiper to be replaced.

Let me tell you of another occasion featuring Assistant Four. As was my practice, I had taken my Youth Fellowship to Troon for a residential conference weekend at Easter. I drove up to Glasgow on the Sunday morning for the morning service, and Assistant Four was to do the same for the evening service. Before he left for the service he checked with me his

proposed praise list and we discovered he had chosen
one hymn that I had used in the morning, 'Christ the
Lord is risen today'. "That's a pity," he said, "I was
particularly keen to have that hymn."

"Well, then," I said, "Go ahead and have it.
The evening congregation is substantially different
from the morning one and in any case there's no law
against singing any hymn both night and morning on
the same day. The organist might not be enthusiastic
but just tell him you particularly want to sing it."

On his return we were all interested to learn
how he had fared.

"The service went well," he said. "Except that
I had some trouble over that hymn."

"Did Sam Thomson demur?" I asked (Sam
being the organist).

"He certainly did," replied Assistant Four.
"When I gave him my praise list, he said immediately
that we'd already sung 'Christ the Lord is risen today'
at the morning service. I told him that I was aware of
that but that I wished to have it sung in the evening as
well and that you had agreed. 'The congregation will
think it very strange,' he muttered, as he went off to
the organ, 'I don't think you should sing it.' "

"When we came to the last hymn," Assistant
Four continued, "I triumphantly announced 'Christ
the Lord is risen today' and sat down waiting for the
organ to start up. But no music came and all I heard
was a scuffling sound from the organ console behind
me. I was just about to turn round to see what was
wrong when I felt a hand tugging my gown. It was
Sam. 'We've already sung that hymn,' he whispered. I
was furious—hadn't we been through all this prior to
the service? 'I know we've sung it already,' I snapped,
'and we're going to sing it again now.' He accepted

defeat then and slunk back to the organ. It was only
after the service that I discovered I had absent-mind-
edly had the congregation sing that hymn to *open* the
service as well as to *close* it."

Assistant Five was somewhat less conven-
tional in the way he dressed for Sunday services than
any of his predecessors had been. No comment was
passed about this until his first communion Sunday
with us when he arrived wearing a plum-coloured
jacket, yellow trousers, green shirt and red tie. At the
first kirk session meeting thereafter, the elders
requested me to suggest as tactfully but nevertheless
as firmly as possible that a more sober style of dress
was their desire for him at the next communion
Sunday—preferably, if possible, a dark suit and white
shirt which was their style of communion wear.

Despite the exceedingly tactful manner in
which I sought to convey their request, Assistant Five
was livid.

"This is what's wrong with the church," he
fulminated. "It's a slave to tradition. They just wear
their white shirts and dark ties because it's always
been done that way. I'm not in favour of formal
dress."

"Don't you agree," I put in mildly, "that there
is a case for the elders all coming dressed in similar
style for the communion occasion—just as, for
instance, people often wear a certain kind of dress for
their wedding?"

"I certainly don't agree. And I don't think
much of people who just conform in matters of dress
whether it's communion or a wedding or anything
else."

A year later, by which time he had moved on
to another church, Assistant Five got married and,

when I met him some time later, he proudly showed me some of his wedding photographs. There he was in full morning dress and topper.

"Goodness gracious," I couldn't help saying. "What happened to the man who was so strongly opposed to conformity in dress?"

"That was different," he protested. "I wore these clothes because I wanted to, not because convention forced me to."

I almost said, "I didn't know that your wife's

name was 'Convention' but that might have been unfair.

Assistants, like apprentices in most spheres, have been the butt of many good jokes. But I look back on mine with a host of fond memories and a depth of gratitude.

Assistants, it is true, sometimes bring headaches with them, but it is the blessings which I remember best. A famous Edinburgh minister once sat for a long time in a parishioner's house, listening to her pour out a tale of unrelieved woe and complaint. When he rose to leave, he said gently, "...and forget not all his benefits."

I gratefully remember many assistant-orientated benefits.

chapter five

here comes the bride

One of the happiest parts of my work as a minister has been the conducting of marriage ceremonies. During my ministry I have had the privilege of conducting almost 1700. Some cynics might reckon that this statistic means that I must constantly feel weighed down beneath a tremendous load of guilt. But in fact I look back on nearly all of my weddings with considerable pleasure.

Apart from anything else, in these days when many more marriages break down than was the case when my ministry began, it is a matter of some satisfaction and encouragement that the vast majority of the marriages I conducted are still going strong.

This reinforces my belief, which I express briefly in some form at every wedding reception over which I preside, that the marriage most likely to succeed is the one which is truly a Christian marriage with each party to it resolved to build on a solid foundation of Christian faith and Christian love.

I could not claim, however, that every wedding service I took ran strictly to plan or to expectations.

I had several which nearly did not take place at all. On two occasions this was due to the absence of the marriage schedule, the presence of which is abso-

lutely essential before the marriage can proceed. It was
my invariable practice, in the course of my final pre-
marriage meeting with the couple, to attempt to
impress upon them the fact that the schedule must be
brought to me on the day of the wedding, otherwise
the wedding simply could not proceed. On these two
occasions I clearly failed miserably in that attempt.

On the first occasion, as was normal practice,
the bridegroom and his best man were ushered into
my vestry some ten minutes before the time
appointed for the marriage to take place. In response
to my welcome, the bridegroom said cheerfully, "By
the way, I don't suppose that the paper you were
speaking about that we got from the registrar really
needs to be here."

"It certainly does," I replied, with a sense of
imminent doom. "I tried to make that plain. Don't you
have it with you?"

"No, I've left it at home. I had so much else to
think about, you know."

"Well," I had to tell him, "I'm afraid you'll
have to go back for it because I can't go on with the
wedding until it is here. It would be illegal."

He obviously thought this was a case of
unnecessary red tape. But the law is perfectly clear on
this point, and unbending. Home he had to go and
since home was about twelve miles away, that was
one wedding which took place somewhat later in the
day than planned—and through no fault of the bride
who turned up on time and had to be 'entertained' in
another part of the church premises until the bridegroom returned with the required document.

The second occasion was even more serious
and it appeared for a long time as if the wedding
would not be able to take place at all that day. It was a

glorious Saturday afternoon in June. The sky was blue, the sun was shining brilliantly and the church was filled, because not only was there a large number of guests but, since both bride and bridegroom stayed very near to the church, many neighbours and friends were there to join in the service.

When I asked the bridegroom for the schedule, he said, "Oh, Maureen has it. She'll be bringing it." This was unusual, and a little inconvenient, since it meant that I had to go round and intercept the bride before she entered the church in order to obtain from her (or her father, more likely) the so essential authorisation.

When she arrived, right on time, I whispered, "Ian tells me you have the marriage schedule. Could I have it now?"

"I don't have it," she said. "I thought Ian had it."

Consternation all round. Back to Ian, back to Maureen, back and forth. Eventually, not without some difficulty, I managed to establish that there was, as a matter of fact, no marriage schedule. They had not even been to the registrar's, as required. It was in the days when banns of marriage still had to be proclaimed and somehow they had the idea that the certificate of proclamation was all that was needed—not that they had brought it to the church either.

It was impossible to proceed without a marriage schedule and only a registrar could issue that document. But it was Saturday afternoon, the registrar's office was closed and there seemed no way out. At length, however, after telephoning round all the registrars I knew, I was fortunate enough to locate one who was at home and was prepared to help us out. The bridegroom and the best man went off to see him, the all important schedule was obtained and some two hours late the wedding took place.

From that time on I insisted that, whenever possible, the marriage schedule should be brought to me *before* the day of the wedding.

I had another wedding that took place two *days* late. All seemed perfectly well in the pre-wedding arrangements but it was nothing short of catastrophic on the day. The bride and her father arrived at the church on time—but the bridegroom never appeared.

The best man had called at his flat (where he lived alone) at the time they had arranged, but could get no reply. Try as he might he could not find the bridegroom anywhere. Nor did he appear on his own at the church. We waited and waited but to no avail. Eventually the broken-hearted bride and her irate father had to go back home; and I dispersed the congregation as diplomatically as I could.

The absent bridegroom turned up the following day. His explanation was that he had had a blackout in his flat and had lain unconscious most of the day. The bride's father was somewhat sceptical and it was with a marked lack of enthusiasm that he brought his daughter back to the church on the following Monday afternoon for me to perform the delayed ceremony. But, happily, the marriage was a success.

I once had a wedding ceremony of sorts without a bridegroom present. It created a considerable interest among the national newspapers and I had telephone calls about it from newspaper men all over the United Kingdom. But it was all a simple matter of pastoral compassion.

One of our High Carntyne girls, Mary Dickie, working in Hawaii and engaged to be married to a United States navyman stationed there, had arranged

with me to be married in her home church. She flew home some weeks ahead in order to complete her wedding preparations and her bridegroom was to come just a few days beforehand. But six days before the wedding, Mary received a telegram from Carl informing her that owing to the Vietnam crisis (this was 1964) all leave had been cancelled and he was unable, therefore, to journey to Glasgow. Mary for her part had to return to the States in less than two weeks time so that it was not possible to find a later date for her to be married in High Carntyne.

Her disappointment was intense at not being able, after all, to be married in High Carntyne, and so, when she asked if some sort of service could be held at the time originally scheduled for the wedding, I was eager to help. I worked out a service which was asking

God's blessing on the marriage which would now take place in Hawaii on Mary's return.

And so it was on an August Saturday in 1964 a limousine drew up at Mary's door to transport her in her bridal gown, escorted by her father, to High Carntyne Church. There, with the organ playing and in presence of the invited guests and many more, they walked down the aisle. With Mary standing before me and her husband-to-be on station in Hawaii, I read some scripture and led the congregation in a prayer for their blessing and for the blessing of the marriage which would take place in Hawaii later on.

Some might reckon that in agreeing to have such a ceremony I was being somewhat naive and over-sentimental. I prefer to regard my action as an act of Christian compassion and potential helpfulness to a couple, and a company of family and friends, who had been the victims of a great disappointment which was not in the least of their making.

Mary flew back to Hawaii as scheduled and a week or two later I received a lovely letter from Carl and her, thanking me for what I had done and informing me that they were now safely and happily married.

Another of my weddings which had a bridegroom attendance problem was resolved by holding the service in the hospital where he was a patient. Three weeks before the day fixed for the marriage, Gordon Hutchison was involved in a head-on car crash at Tyndrum, sustaining a leg broken in two places as well as a broken arm. The leg breaks were so severe that it was reckoned that a three month hospital stay would be required.

At first it seemed that there was no alternative to a lengthy postponement of the wedding, much to the disappointment of Gordon and his fiancee, Carole Dick. Then the young couple had the idea that it might be possible to be married on the agreed date—in hospital. The hospital authorities were agreeable and I was agreeable; and so it was that the marriage ceremony was conducted after all on the original date.

The staff of Glasgow Western Infirmary were simply splendid. They spared no effort to have the setting in the Infirmary Chapel as 'wedding-like' as possible; and the celebration party that followed in Gordon's ward was a very happy affair in spite of everything.

I can honestly say that no two of the weddings I conducted were exactly the same. Of course not, for every wedding is a unique occasion. At the same time, it would be true to say that most of my weddings followed a similar pattern of normality. But not all. Some of them had rather abnormal features.

I remember one wedding which took place at the *sixth* attempt. What I mean is that it actually went through after five postponements. The bridegroom, Roy Edwards, was in the Merchant Navy and sailing in Far Eastern waters. The first date for the wedding was fixed on the basis of what seemed like a sure promise of shore leave. But Roy's ship was on contract to an American firm and based in Japan, and the wedding had to be postponed because the ship which was indeed bound for Britain had to be diverted to Japan. That was in December 1959.

It was actually January 1961 before the wedding finally did take place, and in the interval there had been four other occasions when arrangements were fully made and had to be cancelled because Roy's ship kept getting new sailing orders which in turn kept preventing him getting to Britain. By the time we

came to make the arrangements for the sixth attempt,
Marion Johnstone, the bride-to-be, was almost a nerv-
ous wreck and, I suspect, had little confidence that
things would work out as planned this time either. But
they did—although I had to make a dash from the
reception to the church to collect a passport which had
somehow been left in the vestry, otherwise they
would have missed their honeymoon plane.

That would scarcely qualify for inclusion in
the 'normal' category. Nor would the occasion where I
had a newly married bride and bridegroom sitting in
the church as wedding guests. It was a case of two
sisters being married on the same day but in different
churches. One was, of course, in High Carntyne but
the other was in a neighbouring Roman Catholic
church.

The denomination difference involved made it
impossible to make it a double wedding occasion but
the girls agreed on what seemed to be the next best
thing. They arranged the weddings for the same day
but with a two hour gap between. The girl who was
being married in the Roman Catholic church had her
ceremony first with her sister present in her bridal
attire. After the ceremony everyone bundled into
transport and made their way to my church where the
second wedding took place with the sisters' roles
reversed!

It may have been unusual to have had a bride
in full wedding dress sitting in the pew while I conducted her sister's marriage ceremony in front of the
communion table but it was not nerve-racking either
for the couple standing before me or for me. Not like
the other occasion when the two 'spectators' sitting at
the back of the church were the father and mother of
the bride. They were violently opposed to the mar-

riage and the bride and I were expecting their intervention any moment.

The period before the wedding had been a stormy one so far as the girl and her parents were concerned. From the outset they were convinced that the man she was to marry was a rascal and that she was destined for much trouble and unhappiness. After the wedding arrangements had been made with me by the couple, I had several visits from the parents urging me not to go ahead with the wedding, alleging that they had firm evidence that he was a 'waster'.

I explained that, unless there was some legal impediment to the marriage, and none was known, there was no justification for me to refuse to perform the ceremony, particularly since their daughter insisted that she had complete confidence in her fiance and that her parents' distrust of him was occasioned by nothing other than blind prejudice.

Matters worsened as the wedding date drew nearer. The parents endeavoured with increasing passion but with no more success to dissuade their daughter from going ahead. She grew more and more bitter in her resentment of their attitude and refused even to invite them to the ceremony. At my final meeting with the couple just a few days prior to the wedding day, she warned me that her father had asserted that he would come to the church anyway and she feared it was his intention to voice a protest during the service.

Sure enough he was there, and his wife, too, sitting together at the rear of the church. I always think it a rather dramatic moment when, as I am required to do, I ask if anyone knows any cause to prevent the couple being joined in matrimony. It was especially so that day—but nothing happened. No voice was raised and the service proceeded to its end without interruption.

The bride's father and mother told me later that, strongly though they disapproved, they found themselves unable not to be present to witness their daughter being married and to pray for her happiness.

Unfortunately, their forebodings were proved in only a year or two to be fully justified. In that short space of time the couple broke up and the daughter was back home where, thank God, she was welcomed.

That particular wedding service was not interrupted but I have conducted some that did suffer interruption—not, however, I am pleased and relieved to be able to say, on account of objections raised as to the validity of the proceedings.

One of my weddings was interrupted, and indeed had to be temporarily adjourned, because the bridegroom keeled over in a faint before he had even got to the marriage vows. What a commotion that caused. I had led the bride down the aisle on her father's arm, to take up her position beside her bridegroom. We had sung the opening hymn and I was reading the 'preamble' about the nature of Christian marriage when I observed the bridegroom's colour begin to change. His face grew whiter and whiter and then, suddenly, he slumped to the floor.

I had no alternative but to adjourn the proceedings while we carried him out to the vestry. When he came round somewhat, the best man took him outside and walked him round and round the church while I did my best to reassure and comfort an anxious bride. It was probably only some fifteen minutes later, although it seemed like hours to everyone concerned, before the bridegroom felt able to declare himself fit enough to continue. We all trooped back into the church and I took up the service more or less from the point at which we had broken off.

This time I was able to carry it through to completion without further interruptions. But there was. an unusual—and in my experience, unique— sequel. At the wedding reception the bridegroom again became unwell, and had to go and lie down before we got to the speeches. As a result, when we came to the toast to the newly-weds, the reply was given by the bride!

On that occasion I had a wedding ceremony which was in danger of not being completed. I can remember another which was in danger of not getting *started* and this one was not a matter of participants not turning up nor of papers not being to hand. But I will require to sketch in some background before I tell you of it.

Over my years in High Carntyne there was a detectable change in the nature of many of my wed-dings—perhaps you could call it a secularisation. At least, an increasing number became less 'churchy'.

For most of my time in High Carntyne we had an average of some fifty or more weddings each year. In the first half of my ministry there, most of these weddings were of couples from families in the church and who were often themselves not only brought up in the church but active in its affairs. As the years passed the parish not only aged but to some extent changed its character. The Glasgow housing policy was such that in a housing scheme like ours the young couples I was marrying were unable to rent a house in the scheme and were compelled, therefore, to find accommodation further afield mostly by entering into house ownership. This inevitably drained away much of the vigour and potential leadership from High Carntyne Church.

One consequence was that in the latter half of my ministry, although the number of weddings maintained a level not much short of the earlier days, the proportion of church family weddings began to show a steady decline. In nearly every case still, the young couples themselves attended church regularly. This was in part because I always stressed to them the importance of regular church attendance in making a church wedding what it was meant to be; and most of them responded wholeheartedly. But with increasing frequency I would find on the wedding day that, apart from the bride and bridegroom, few of the wedding congregation were church-goers. This led to some strange experiences for me.

I discovered, for instance, that I could no longer assume that every congregation would know when to stand up and when to sit down. I could no longer count on every congregation being familiar with the hymns. On more than on one occasion the singing was virtually a solo effort from me and I certainly could not claim that that was an enhancement to the worship!

The most bizarre consequence of this 'secularisation' element of my weddings nearly prevented one service from even making a beginning. I was in the vestry and already robed when the church officer burst in in a state of high excitement.

"You'd better come and see this for yourself or you'll never believe it. There's a man standing at the back of the church offering a glass of whisky to each of the guests as they enter."

And so there was. Not only that. By the time I was called in, he had found it too slow and tedious to pour out each glass individually as required and had emptied the whisky bottle into the offering plate which stood just inside the church. As each guest came in, he was scooping up a glassful of whisky and offering it to him or her.

He thought he was making a splendid contribution to the happiness of a happy occasion and it took some very emphatic persuasion on our part to have him desist. In the end, however, he did, although reluctantly. But the church reeked of whisky for days!

chapter six

wedding receptions I have attended

The celebration following the marriage ceremony—mostly referred to as the wedding *reception* in
my area of the country—has also furnished me with a
multitude of varied memories.

The wedding reception is reckoned of great
importance by most people and by some, I fear, of
greater importance than the marriage ceremony itself.
I remember one guest saying to me at a certain wedding reception, "I am sorry I did not get to the church
but I am so glad I have managed to get to the wedding
(sic!)"

I pointed out to him as gently as I was able
that the *wedding* was what had taken place in the
church and what we were now engaged in was the
post-wedding social function which, although of
importance, was of secondary importance to what had
happened in the church earlier that day.

It has always been my practice to attend the
wedding reception when invited, if I was free to do so.
I have done so because I consider it a pastoral service.
It is, I think, of considerable assistance to many that,
as is the norm in the West of Scotland at least, the
minister should preside at the wedding feast and pilot
the participants through the programme of toasts and
speeches to follow.

I also reckon it can be of pastoral value, even of missionary value, in terms of the people met, both church and non-church, in that context. I am hopeful, too, that the word I try to say—brief but to the point—about Christian marriage in the course of my toast to the bride and groom might scatter a seed or two that are worth sowing.

Since I, therefore, found myself attending around fifty wedding receptions a year and since each one would involve me in about a few hours of my time, even though I usually excused myself immediately the meal and the speeches were concluded, this meant the expenditure of some two hundred hours annually. I often asked myself—and still do—if this was a wise expenditure of time. Might I have been using that time to a greater advantage, even pastorally, in other ways?

Not all ministers agree with me. My predecessor took the perfectly justifiable position that he could not afford to spend so much time in this way, and save for the daughters or sons of office-bearers in the church, he did not attend wedding receptions. And there are some who, on principle and quite apart from the time factor, do not accept invitations to the receptions that may follow the weddings they conduct. I remember once being severely taken to task on this very matter.

He was a young minister in his first charge, with a congregation about one quarter the size of mine, and we were attending the same conference. Somehow during one of the coffee breaks, we got into conversation about wedding receptions.

"On principle I never go to any," he affirmed. "I simply could not spare the time in any case."

"Do you have a large number of weddings?" I

asked, as the troublesome question was again raised in my mind as to whether or not the time I spent at wedding receptions was wasted.

"Last year I had six," he answered. "That's about the usual. How about you?"

"Last year I had nearly sixty," I was forced to admit. "And I am afraid I attended about fifty of the receptions."

"That's a ridiculous waste of time!" he declared. "You won't catch me doing that."

Although he was my junior both in years and in experience, I was by now—to my internal annoyance—feeling rather discomfited, and I hastened to try and defend myself.

"I like to think," I submitted, "that I am being of some pastoral service to the bridal party by being there and piloting them through the speeches and that sort of thing."

That remark served to make him even more dismissive of my policy. "That attitude," he declared forcibly, "I find very insulting to the people concerned. It's as if to say that they would not be able to cope on their own."

When I reflected on it, I found some comfort in my conviction that the fact was that some of them certainly would *not* have coped on their own.

That young minister, by the way, gave up the ministry the very next year. I do not know the reason except that it was *not* due to a surfeit of wedding receptions.

I must admit that attendance at wedding receptions has involved me in some wearisome hours and some frustrating ones. But it has provided me with many enriching moments and many happy memories, too; and some less usual ones.

There was the time, for instance, when I was button-holed by a guest as soon as I had entered the hotel where the reception was being held. "I just want you to know," he said, "that I don't believe any of that Christian rubbish. I don't see how any intelligent man could be taken in by it."

"I am sorry to hear you say that," I replied, "for you are missing a great deal in life that is there for you to take. I obviously can't enter into a discussion about it now. All I can say is that *I* believe it, otherwise I wouldn't be here."

That rather aggressive approach was far from typical. Usually, whether people are believers or church-goers or not, they are polite and kindly to the poor clergyman who is in a kind of no-man's-land, belonging neither to the bride's side nor the groom's. Very often indeed the guests who have little or no active connection with any church may go to great lengths to find some common ground.

"My mother had a second cousin who was a minister."

"How interesting. What was his name? Where was his church?"

"I just can't remember his name, I am afraid, but I think he had a church somewhere in the North of Scotland."

Mind you, getting to the reception was not always the simple, smooth operation one would normally expect it to be. One of the first group of weddings I performed in High Carntyne was an illustration of that. Those were the days before I owned a car and the arrangement made by the bride was that I would travel to the reception with the ushers, Alex Donnan and Alistair Gardener. They were two very tall, handsome lads in their later teens who were resplendent in their 'tails' and all the accompanying wedding finery.

The plan was that they would see all the guests into the cars and off to the reception; and then, satisfied that no one had been left behind without transport, they would escort me in the last car to the hotel. When I emerged from the vestry after disrobing and tidying up there, it was to see the ushers waving off the last of the guests.

"I can see you've done a very good job," I remarked, "as well as looking quite splendid. Now let's get into our car and follow on."

At that their faces changed colour simultaneously and spectacularly.

"Oh," they gulped in unison, "we've forgotten to keep back a car for our own use. That's the last of them just turning the corner now."

It took a few seconds for the full impact of the situation to dawn on me, and then I made a determined effort to appear more philosophical about their gaffe than I really felt.

"Well, we've got to get to the reception," I said brightly, "and the service buses go very close to the hotel. We'll just hop on to one of them."

That suggestion was strangled at birth. In the same unison as before my male chorus of two exclaimed, "What? In this gear? You must be joking!" And no plea or persuasion would move them. For them to use public transport dressed as they were seemed like a fate worse than death. Why, they might even be seen by someone who knew them.

"Right, then," I said at last, conceding defeat, "I'll go and ask Mr. Armit, the chemist, if I can use his phone and try to get a taxi from somewhere." And off I went to Mr. Armit's shop, across the square from the

church, and explained our predicament. But Alex
Armit refused to allow me to telephone for a taxi.
Instead he bundled the three of us into his own car
and drove us to the reception where our non-arrival
was just beginning to cause a bit of anxiety.

I was relieved to note later that their experience had not unduly upset Alex and Alistair, not at
any rate if I were to judge by the enormous helpings of
food they consumed.

Despite the transport hiccup, I did get to that
wedding reception, and in plenty of time. But there
was another which in my pre-car days I missed
altogether, that of Joyce Higgins and Andrew Aitken.
The arrangements made for my transportation to the
reception were most satisfactory, very precise and
spelled out beforehand in exact detail. One of the
ushers was to take me with him in the last car to leave,
this giving me time to disrobe (I perhaps ought to
have recognised that this script was dangerously similar to that previous one).

Once I had escorted the bridal party through
the church and out of the front door, I wasted no time
in doubling back to the vestry, taking off my robes
and making my way once again to the front of the
church to join the car. But others had been even
quicker. It was a wet afternoon in late December and it
was already pitch dark by the time the service was
over. Consequently, there were practically no photographs at the church door and speed was the order of
the day as the guests piled into the cars to follow the
bridal party to the reception.

So much speed, in fact, that, when I arrived at
the front door of the church, I was in time only to see
the tail-lights of the last car (with usher inside) rapidly

disappearing from view. Our church officer was engaged in closing the church gates.

"Is there another car still to go, Johnny?" I asked.

"No, Mr. Martin. That's the last one. I thought you couldn't be going because I heard someone say 'Are you sure that's everyone?' and the usher said, 'Yes, I've checked. That's them all,' and off they went."

"The trouble is, Johnny, that I wasn't told where the reception is being held so I can't make my own way. However, provided they haven't a long distance to travel, I suppose they'll soon discover what has happened and someone will come back for me. I'll just go back to the vestry and wait till they come."

Well, I waited and waited and waited. After about an hour and a half I decided that, whatever the reason, no one *was* going to come for me. In any case, since I had to attend a church function later in the evening, I calculated that unless I were to go to it hungry, I required now to find myself some food. Off I went to do just that and I never was at that wedding reception, even though it was one that for a number of reasons I was particularly anxious to attend.

It turned out that, in the darkness and the wet, it was not so much that I had been forgotten but that I had been assumed to be safely ensconced in someone else's car—or so the ushers claimed, perhaps to save me the feeling of humiliation at just being forgotten. At the reception it was only after all the photographs had been taken, other preliminaries had been attended to and the top table party was being seated for the meal that my absence came to light. When it was eventually ascertained that I had been left behind at the church, a car was dispatched post-haste in what

everyone realised was now a forlorn hope that I might still be there. But to no avail.

Despite that unfortunate and naturally disappointing episode, the young couple and I continued to be good friends; and, I am happy to say, remain so to this day. But it did cause one change in my pre-marriage procedure. From that time on, when I was invited to attend a wedding reception, I always asked where it was to take place and wrote it in my diary at once—realising as I did so that I was risking a reaction like, "Does this guy consent to come only if the venue is to his liking?"

I discovered once that, even carefully writing down the name of the hotel or whatever, was not an absolute guarantee that I would, under my own steam, arrive at the correct place—not with *my* handwriting. After I acquired a car, my invariable practice was to drive myself to the reception. On the occasion in question I had another wedding to perform after the one whose reception I had agreed to attend, so that I was prepared for the likelihood of the company being ready or almost ready to begin the meal by the time I arrived. I had a quick look at my diary to refresh my memory as to where the reception was being held, I said to myself, "Ah, yes, the Grand Hotel," jumped into my car and headed across the city to what was a popular location for wedding receptions.

When I arrived and enquired where my wedding reception was, I was directed to the appropriate suite with the remark, "You've timed it nicely, sir, the bridal party are just receiving their guests now." So I scuttled up the stairs and attached myself to the end of the queue of people standing in the corridor waiting their turn to be formally announced to the bridal party ready to receive them inside the banqueting room.

As I waited, I chatted with the people next to me. I did not recognise a single one of them but that was not surprising. By the nature of the case, very many of the guests at any wedding I conducted were likely to be strangers to me. Slowly the queue moved nearer to the open door and in due course I was able to see the bridal party within. To my horror, I did not recognise any of them either. With dismay I realised that this was *not* my wedding.

Excusing myself as diplomatically as I could, I detached myself from the group and made my way down the stairs and back to the desk. "That's not my wedding reception in suite so-and-so," I said. "Where will I find mine?"

"That, sir, is the only reception we have in the hotel tonight."

"Are you sure?"

"Positive."

Again I excused myself as gracefully as I could and fled to the privacy of my car. How could I have written down the wrong hotel? Where could the reception be? What was I to do? Telephone round all the hotels in Glasgow till I hit upon the one I wanted?

As I worked myself into an increasing lather of frustration and anxiety, I took out my diary and looked at the entry once more, hoping against hope it might supply some clue. I looked more closely and still more closely. "That's not *Grand* Hotel, I've written there, is it? Surely it is *George* Hotel."

George Hotel it was, less than ten minutes drive away—and when I got there, my wedding reception—yes, it was mine this time—was just at the stage at which I had blundered upon the other one. No one ever knew how daft I had been. So all was well in the end—but, supposing I myself had not noticed my mistake before I was in the room, shaking hands with the parents and so on, would I have been expelled in disgrace as a gatecrasher, perhaps to crawl away and die in shame? Or would I—and I have often wondered if this would have been the more likely outcome—would I simply have been accepted as an unexpected guest who must, of course, belong to the 'other side'?

chapter seven

ashes to ashes

Marriages are among the most pleasant tasks I have had to perform as a minister. Funerals, on the other hand, were, of course, among the saddest; and I have had even more of them—over two thousand, as a matter of fact. In my later years at High Carntyne, as the parish population aged, the number of weddings dropped off a little but the number of funerals increased dramatically. In my last four or five years there I was conducting around 120 or more funerals each year.

This was obviously an increasing burden, not only nor even chiefly in terms of the high cost in man hours (each funeral involving as it did, as a minimum, a visit to the bereaved house before the funeral, the funeral itself, and a visit to the house after the funeral) but especially in terms of the escalating cost spiritually and emotionally. This kind of cost seemed to increase in direct proportion to the length of time I had known the family involved. I consoled myself with the hope that, as a long association with the family concerned in a bereavement situation meant that the burden I carried was that much heavier as a result, it also might mean that I was able to be an instrument of greater help and comfort.

Never did I hope and pray more fervently that

that might be so as when Carole Harper died suddenly and tragically. I had known her father and mother since their teens, had seen them become stalwarts in my Youth Fellowship, had admitted them to church membership, had married them, and had baptised their children.

Carole had not only grown into a lovely young woman by the time she reached her twenty-first birthday but was also showing considerable talent, especially in the field of fine art. In the summer of 1986, when our younger daughter was to be married, Carole designed and made a wedding dress for her—an exquisite creation it was as even a mere male could tell—and she was one of the guests at the happy event itself.

It was only a few weeks later that I answered the telephone early one morning to hear Carole's mother say, "Carole is dead."

It seemed impossible and at first my mind tried to reject it. But it was true. Through the night Carole suffered an asthma attack and this, combined with a latent influenza infection, took her life within the hour.

My close personal involvement and long association with the family combined with the tragic circumstances meant that Carole's was one of the most difficult and most harrowing funeral services I ever had to conduct. At the same time I believe that the extent to which these factors added to the weight of the burden I was called to bear may in some degree have been paralleled by the greater help and support I was therefore able to give.

I hope so, at any rate, for that belief was at times all that kept me going through the nearly two thousand funeral services I had to conduct in High

Carntyne. Few could approach the peculiar poignancy of Carole's but all had their own sadness and a considerable number had their own pathos and drama, too.

There was the young lad who just a month earlier stood before me in his R.A.F. uniform to take his marriage vows and now had lost his life when his plane crashed.

There were the infant twins whose parents' grief was almost unbearable to witness.

There was the young husband and father who answered the door at night to be struck down and killed by a drunken hooligan.

There was the devoted family of daughter, father and mother whose funerals followed each other at regular intervals.

There was the young mother who died of cancer leaving behind three children under five years of age.

A particularly tragic case was the accidental death of ten-year-old Christine Mason. A vivacious and talented child, she was a member of our Junior Choir which met for rehearsal on Friday evenings. One Friday evening when I dropped in to see them at their practice, I found that Christine was not present. We assumed she must be ill because she was never known to miss a choir night.

But it was much worse than that, as I soon discovered. A message came to the church asking me to call—urgently—at Christine's home. I went at once and encountered a scene of utter devastation. Christine had been home from school about one hour before her parents arrived. When they entered the house, it was to find her dead. She had been playing around with the pulley rope suspended from the kitchen ceiling, and had somehow got her head entangled in it. Her mother and father came upon her hanging from it, choked to death.

That also was a funeral which affected almost the whole of the congregation. So did many others; and all of them carried their own quota of sadness.

But it was not all sadness. Sadness was always present and often was there in very large measure; but just as often there were other things too, particularly where the mourners were possessed of genuine Christian faith. On those occasions there were courage and strength and even serenity as well.

There were some, however, that contained an almost unbearable volume of sheer pathos. A few of these came into my purview on account of my being chaplain to Lightburn, a small 120-bed geriatric hospital situated close to my parish of High Carntyne.

On one occasion I was asked to conduct a funeral service for a patient who had no known relatives. It was arranged, as was the usual practice in such circumstances, that some of the hospital staff would attend the service, which was to be only a short ceremony at the graveside. We turned up at the cemetery at the appointed time, but our dead friend did not. The funeral had been postponed for a day but the deceased apparently mattered so little to anyone that no one had troubled to inform us. Of course I felt some irritation at the unnecessary waste of my time; but to a considerable extent, more did I feel the awfulness of a man departing this life with so little real personal interest being shown in him.

I experienced similar emotions the day I conducted the funeral of another lonely patient. On this occasion, owing to staff shortages, no one from the hospital could be present and the congregation that joined with me in the service I conducted at the crematorium consisted of the undertaker and the crematorium attendant.

The one that affected me most poignantly of all the 'lonely' funerals I conducted was Emily's, no doubt because she and I had developed a real friendship during her years in the hospital. Blind, and without any living relatives, she would have presented a very pathetic figure had it not been for her indomitable courage and her firm Christian faith. She never missed attending my weekly Sunday afternoon service in the hospital and, despite many periods of acute illness, always managed to 'count her blessings'.

One day the ward sister telephoned me to say that Emily had died and asked me if I could take her funeral service. She explained that, since there were no known relatives, the hospital administrator would have to make the arrangements and, because of the circumstances, this might mean some delay.

I was, therefore, not surprised that a week passed without my being informed of the funeral arrangements, although it was rather longer than is normal in Scotland between a death and the funeral. On the eighth morning after Emily's death, I had just returned from a visit to the church when the 'phone rang. It was twenty minutes to ten and on the other end of the line was an undertaker whom I knew well.

"Did anyone speak to you about Emily's funeral?"

"Oh, yes," I replied, "I agreed to do it—and willingly, because she and I were good friends. Have the arrangements been made?"

"Yes, they have," he said, "I am afraid there's been a slip up. Someone should have told you. It's today."

"Today?" I replied, "What time?"

"It was supposed to be at 9.30. We're here at the crematorium and I realised something must be wrong when you did not turn up on time."

I was utterly dismayed for I wanted so much to take the service myself and I knew that would have been Emily's wish.

Conscious that it was nearly twenty minutes drive to the crematorium and that I was dressed casually; and conscious too, that it would be unusual if the crematorium did not have another service scheduled for 10 o'clock, I nevertheless said, "I'm prepared to come right away just as I am, if there's no service due at 10 and if you're able to wait."

To my surprise and relief, he said, "The next service due is at 10.30 and we're prepared to wait till you come."

I broke all records, I think, to get there as quickly as possible and so was able to conduct the service for Emily in the presence of the undertaker and three friends of hers.

What a contrast there was between these almost solitary funerals and the many hundreds I conducted where the funeral parlours and the crematoria were packed with mourners. I had one for which ten thousand turned out to mourn. That was Jock Stein's, perhaps the most famous of all the football managers Scotland has ever produced.

Jock died suddenly and tragically at the end of a World Cup match in Cardiff when Scotland dramatically qualified for the final stages at the expense of their immediate opponents, Wales. As a friend of his, I was invited to conduct his funeral service which took place a few days later at the Linn Crematorium in Glasgow. The service, at the family's request, was to be on a modest scale, despite Jock's fame, and not open to the public. Even at that, with the family and family friends, football friends and dignitaries, the crematorium chapel was crammed full and even had people standing.

But by far the most impressive, and most moving, feature of the day was the huge crowd of the ordinary people of Glasgow who turned up to line the route along which the cortege passed to the crematorium. To a man (and a woman, for there were many women among the crowds) the Glasgow people respected the expressed wish of the family that Jock Stein's funeral should not be made into any kind of circus or flamboyant spectacle. Not one, except those invited or expected to attend, encroached on the crematorium chapel or even on the crematorium grounds.

But they massed in thousands—ten thousand of them, at least, was the police estimate of those standing to pay their sorrowful respects along the nearer approaches to the Linn. For my part, as we drove to Jock Stein's last resting place, I found it intensely moving to see the massive crowds flanking the roads, five and six deep, and many of them clearly dressed in their best clothes for the occasion.

Despite the inevitable sadness and solemnity that must be part of any and of every funeral, not a few of the funerals I conducted had elements of humour, too; and some were almost hilarious in a bizarre kind of fashion. These were often in situations where the chief mourners had little or no church connection and possibly even less religion.

On one such occasion, in the course of the service I was conducting in the crematorium chapel, I said in my prayer, "We thank you, O God, that Jesus still has the power to bring Lazarus from the grave to new life." Suddenly the deceased's brother, sitting in the front row, shouted out, "His name wisnae Lazarus. It wis Wullie!"

That brother may have been giving himself some measure of 'spiritual' stimulation before the funeral, a practice which was not unknown and which sometimes had embarrassing consequences. At times I have known it to lead to excessive fidgetting, audible conversation and even loud interjections (not always of a reverent character) during the service, short though it usually was.

I remember the crematorium attendant once whispering to me as I went to greet the chief mourner whom he had just led in, "Don't go too near him or his breath might make you drunk." There was another service I had where the chief mourners—the husband and son of the deceased—were both heavily intoxicated. The son talked most of the way through the service which I nevertheless tried to conduct with as much dignity and helpfulness as I could. When it was over, the father came forward to me at once and for a moment I thought that he wished to apologise for his son's behaviour.

But he was bent on a different errand. In the Church of Scotland there are no fees for performing pastoral duties, such as funerals. Not infrequently, however, those to whom the pastoral service is rendered may make a gift to the minister or to his church. It turned out that something of this was in his somewhat befuddled brain. "The Post Office is shut," he blurted out, as he grasped my hand, "The Post Office is shut and ah'm skint, but ah'll see you later."

His next spoken contribution to the proceedings was equally memorable. After the service, which took place in the funeral parlour, we went to the cemetery for the burial. Our practice at a burial is that the coffin is lowered slowly and reverently into the grave by cords attached to it at different points and held by the eight nearest relatives or friends. When, at the graveside, the undertaker offered the widowed husband cord number one, he declined it. Then he turned to a woman standing near and said, "Ah'm no taking a cord. Ah might fall into the bluidy grave."

Having to cope with circumstances such as these could add considerably to the undoubted strain of conducting a funeral service. Anxiety about remembering the name of the deceased was at times a factor, too, when he or she had not been personally known to me. However, the longer I was in High Carntyne the more likely it was that when I had a funeral to conduct it would be of someone I not only knew but knew well. That was why I had no trouble—not so far as the names were concerned, anyway—the afternoon I took five services in non-stop succession at Daldowie Crematorium. In the space of two hours, by dint of shuttling back and forth between the West Chapel and the East, I conducted all five and had no difficulty with any of the names—because I knew all of them personally.

I was fortunate, also, that in spite of the large number of funerals at which I officiated, I never experienced confusion of mind during the service as to the sex of the deceased. I thank God for that because it is a whole lot easier than it may appear to find oneself in such a situation and one or two of my friends have endured great agony in mind because they simply could not remember, when the time of the committal arrived, whether they should be saying 'his' body or 'her' body.

One colleague, finding himself in just such a position, attempted to save the day very adroitly. It was a 'parish' funeral, that is, one to which he had been called because the family resided in his church's area, although they had never had any connection with him or his congregation. And in this particular instance he had been unable to make any personal contact with the family beforehand. To his horror he realised as he was about to begin the service that he did not even know whether the dead person was a man or a woman. With great presence of mind, he turned to the chief mourner and asked with appropriate solemnity, "Will you announce, please, the name of your departed loved one"?

When the mourner, suitably impressed, announced, "Evelyn," my friend found himself none the wiser as to the sex of the deceased and somehow got through the whole service without ever using a masculine or feminine term. The service, however, must have lost a lot as a result, in terms of warmth and intimacy.

Sometimes there were lighter moments connected with funerals that were quite apart from the funeral service itself. I arrived at Daldowie Crematorium one day to find the attendants rolling about laughing at the rather bizarre misfortunate that had overtaken the undertaker who had been directing the funeral immediately prior to the one I was to conduct.

It had been a Roman Catholic funeral and, consequently, a number of Mass Cards had been placed on the top of the coffin. The service had gone through without any hitch, and, as usual, with the pronouncing of the words of committal, the coffin had been discreetly and with dignity conveyed on the rollers from the catafalque through the partition to the area of the furnace. Then the mourners left the chapel, got into their cars and dispersed.

Five minutes later the undertaker burst into the chapel, considerably agitated. "I hope I'm in time," he cried. "By mistake I've put amongst the Mass Cards an envelope containing £50 as a gift for the priest." But it was too late. The coffin and the cards and the letter were already in the furnace—and the £50 was beyond recall.

That is a perfectly true story, as I can testify. But I suppose that there have been as many, if not more, jokes invented about deaths and funerals as about any other subject. I want to share one with you.

The doctor was examining a patient lying motionless in his bed at home. Shaking his head sadly, the doctor turned to the man's wife and said, "I'm afraid he is dead." At that the man in the bed whispered, "No, I'm not, I'm still alive.""Keep quiet," his wife said. "Don't contradict the doctor. He knows best."

As weddings have been amongst the happiest part of my work, so funerals have been amongst the saddest. But they have not been unrelieved sadness. And I for my part have tried, in every one of these thousands of funeral services I have conducted, to affirm the comforting message that the Christian Gospel emphatically contradicts any assertion that death must be the end.

chapter eight

baptisms

As with marriages and funerals, baptisms are an integral part of the on-going work of the parish minister; and so it was with me. Like my marriages and funerals, I had many, many more baptisms in High Carntyne than in Newmilns owing to the simple fact that my congregation and parish were immensely larger in the one than in the other. I performed more baptisms in a year in High Carntyne than during my whole time in Newmilns. But like the marriages and the funerals, all were of equal importance wherever they took place and whoever might be involved.

I suppose that for every minister baptisms belong to the happier side of his work. I certainly have a multitude of happy memories in regard to the many hundreds of baptisms I performed, a large number outstandingly so. But even baptisms sometimes brought headaches.

Our normal Church of Scotland practice is baptism in infancy, although provision is made for the baptism of adults where baptism has not previously been administered, for whatever reason. Most years I had several adult baptisms as well as a large number of infant baptisms.

It was usually because of my endeavours—in

common with most of my fellow ministers—to observe the correct procedures that difficulties sometimes arose. The Church of Scotland requires that when a child is presented for baptism at least one of the parents must have an active connection with the church. I always tried to adhere to this. Where such an active connection already existed there was rarely any problem. Where it did not, I had to attempt to ensure that it was established, or that a reliable promise was given that it would be, before proceeding to the baptism. This was the point at which problems were most likely to arise.

Some people simply could not, or would not, understand why there should be such a fuss about church attendance and the like. All they wanted was that their baby should be 'done'. They did not see that for the baby to be 'done' properly, that is, for the baptism to be what it was meant to be, there had to be vows taken and kept by them involving matters like attendance at church and Christian training and example. Sometimes there was resentment when I pointed out that a parental commitment was necessary before the baptism could proceed. At times that resentment spilled over into vituperation.

I remember one new father, totally unknown to me, who came along to my vestry hour one Monday evening. "My wife and I want you to christen our baby," he said. "I will be very happy to do that," I replied, "but first of all I have to satisfy myself that you are prepared to accept the commitment involved. Since I do not know you, I take it that you do not come to church. Does your wife?"

"No, neither of us has ever attended church."

"One of you at least—preferably both of you—will need to start attending and promise to keep

attending, otherwise I cannot baptise your baby, much as I would like to. How about it?"

"Certainly not," he declared. "We're not interested in coming to church. We just want our baby christened. What's attending church got to do with that?"

"That's the Church law," I replied. "And a good one. In offering your child for baptism you are asked to make certain promises so that the child will be brought up to be a Christian. It's impossible to keep these promises and at the same time show no interest in the Church. As I've said, I'll be very happy to baptise your baby if you're prepared to take the vows, which mean coming to church as well as other things, so it's really up to you."

"We'll not be wasting our time coming to church," he spat out. "We just want the baby christened. But if you'll not do it, I'll just go and look for someone who will."

He got out of his chair, the interview clearly at an end, and realising that I could make no impression on him, I escorted him to the door. As he was leaving, a number of people were arriving for various meetings that were soon to start. I do not know whether or not it was the prospect of an audience that stimulated him. In any event he suddenly turned on his heel, a few yards away from me and began to shout at the top of his voice. "Call yourself a Christian, do you? And yet you refuse to christen my child. Fine Christian you are!"

On occasion I found the task of upholding the Church regulations regarding baptism was made both more difficult and more embarrassing by the fact that there tends to be a 'rogue' minister here and there who simply thumbs his nose at regulations.

I remember one young couple coming to me to have their baby baptised. Neither attended church, although the wife's mother was a 'regular'. I explained that I was not free to perform the ceremony unless one of them, if not both, was prepared to start attending and they went away promising to come back the following week after thinking about it.

They failed to appear the next week, and the next again; and so the following Sunday I enquired of the mother, "Your daughter hasn't come back to see me about the baptism. Is there anything wrong?"

"Nothing wrong," she came back, almost malevolently. "The baby's been baptised. Mr. Kennedy in the next parish did it without asking any questions."

I recall another very similar incident. A young mother had been to my vestry requesting that her baby should be baptised and I had responded in the same way as before. She promised to start attending church the next Sunday and to come back to the next vestry night along with her husband so that we might make the arrangements for the baptism. When she failed to appear at either, I telephoned her, only to be informed that the child had already been baptised— again by a neighbouring minister, only this time it was one who was actually a member of the Presbytery's Superintendence Committee, part of whose remit was to ensure that matters like baptism should be carried out according to the regulations.

Ministers like that, who cock a snook at the recognised procedures, often make life difficult for the majority of us who try honestly to keep to the rules. But it is not only ministers who can aggravate the problem. I had an elder, a good friend and faithful churchman he was, who maintained vigorously at one kirk session meeting that every baby should be baptised without any conditions at all.

"Why should the child suffer because of the regulations?" he asked.

"But," I protested, "it's precisely in order to avoid the child suffering that the regulations have been made. Baptism is about bringing the baptised child into the fellowship of the Church and ultimately into personal Christian faith. It is to ensure that everything may be done that will help towards that end that the prescribed commitment of one or both parents is required before the child is baptised. To go ahead willy-nilly whether or not the parents are prepared to do anything about it is a recipe for disaster and makes it much less likely that the aims of baptism will be

achieved so far as that particular child is concerned. So you see," I continued in my patient way, "it's for the child's good, not for its harm, that I follow the rules laid down."

He was quite unimpressed by my masterly explanation.

"I don't see it that way at all,' he came back, "and I think it's dreadful that any minister should turn away a child from the Church, when Jesus himself said that he wanted the little children to come to him."

I tried again.

"It's entirely because I want to help the little children find their way to Jesus that I insist on the parental commitment that the regulations demand for that very purpose. And I would deny that I have ever turned away an infant knowingly. I always make it plain that I welcome the opportunity to baptise the child and will be only too happy to do so provided the parents are prepared to do their part. If, in the end, the child is not brought forward to be baptised by me, the refusal is the parents', not mine."

Despite what seemed to me the spell-binding quality of my defence, my elder remained unconvinced. I was very sorry about that because he and I were very good friends; but I continued to do things in the manner I saw as right. And it certainly did not affect our friendship.

Most baptisms were straight-forward and free from controversy. And every one was delightful in its own way because, of course, every baby is delightful in its own way. This does not mean that conducting a baptism was always an effortless and undemanding task. It was always something that exacted its price, as must be the case with anything and everything that is worth doing.

Sometimes, however, baptisms had their lighter moments, too. One of the factors that could cause a feeling of some anxiety was the responsibility of remembering and using the correct names for the baby or babies being baptised. I happened to be pretty good at this and I never failed to get them exactly right, even the Sunday morning that I had no less than nine babies to baptise!

While I had every confidence in my memory, most times I used to play safe by confirming sotto-voce with the father as I took the baby from him. One Sunday I took the child from his father and whispered, "George John?"

"No, Walter James."

Fortunately, I realised just in time that he had misunderstood and was nervously and no doubt in some bewilderment giving me his *own* name.

chapter nine

preaching the word

I belong to what some might term the old-fashioned school of thought which believes and believes firmly that preaching is not only an essential but an extremely important part of the minister's task.

All through my ministry preaching has been one of the most awesome and yet one of the most thrilling aspects of my job. It was able also to afford me on some occasions tremendous personal uplift and on others to be the very effective medium of the pricking of the bubbles of my self-esteem.

Someone once said that there is never any true preaching without the shedding of blood. It was perhaps a highly dramatised way to put it but I both understand and endorse what he was getting at. In my own experience I certainly found it profoundly true that preaching can be a costly and demanding thing. Not just in terms of the effort required to prepare a sermon—although that can often be strenuous enough—but even more in terms of the price exacted by the awareness of the awful responsibility that lies with the preacher of the Gospel every time he takes his place in the pulpit or on the platform.

If he is committed to his task—and he ought not to be occupying a pulpit unless he is—the preacher is aware that what he is commissioned to communicate is far and away the most important message in all history, the Good News of God's love and of eternal life made available through faith in Jesus Christ. It is inevitable then that every occupancy of pulpit or platform will be an occasion of considerable tension, strain and cost.

To look on a congregation, whether it is numbered in handfuls or in hundreds or in thousands, and to know that you are the spokesman to them of what is no less than a matter of life and death, is to know also that you carry an awesome burden of prestige and of responsibility.

This may explain why intermittently throughout my ministry I had a horrific nightmare in which I found myself in the pulpit facing a packed church and had no sermon to deliver. Sometimes I was simply caught unprepared, mostly I had somehow left my sermon notes behind. Either way I was there before that huge congregation, all of them looking at me in expectation of my sermon—and I did not have anything to say. "The hungry sheep looked up and were not fed"—and I was engulfed with a dreadful feeling of shame and horror.

It is that same awful feeling of shame and horror which assails the conscientious preacher whenever he feels that, whatever the causes, the hungry people are looking to him and he is failing to feed them. I experienced that feeling many a time, and so I am well aware that the burden of preaching can be a very heavy one to carry.

At the same time, I enjoyed preaching and it has given me not a little satisfaction and a lot of fun.

Scots Church folk are not usually given to an over-indulgence in spoken praise of their minister's preaching even when it is to their liking. Mostly it is just accepted in silence. From the minister's point of view this is a great pity because most of us are none the worse of a word of appreciation and encouragement now and again. I have often felt that, if Church people were more aware of how words of thanks might help their minister along his way, many more would be spoken.

As things are, most of the time when preaching is acceptable it is largely taken for granted. This can be a bit disappointing and even discouraging for the minister but it does serve to make the occasions when appreciative words are spoken both more uplifting and more memorable. When a minister is told that a sermon of his has led to a blossoming of faith and a transformation of life, that makes all the 'shedding of blood' well worthwhile.

I mention two such experiences of my own by way of illustration. One of my very enthusiastic elders in High Carntyne was Jamie Stuart who became well known throughout Scotland and beyond for his writing and presentation of 'A Scots Gospel'. When I came to High Carntyne his attachment to the church was slender and he used often to recall to me how it was a sermon I preached when he attended a church service following his father's funeral, that sent a "shaft of Light into his soul and led him to the feet of Jesus".

I treasure that and other Carntyne memories, as I do many more preaching-related memories that belong to other places. The second one I promised to tell you about has its geographical location in Berlin.

I was in Berlin in the course of a lightning preaching tour of U.S. military bases in Europe—to preach and talk to Berlin-based American service personnel. When the military wife who was presiding over the large gathering introduced me, one of the things she said took me by delighted surprise. "I owe my life in the Lord to a sermon I heard the Rev. Martin preach ten months ago in Berchtesgaden."

Indeed I treasure the memory of such comments but I carry in my memory a number of others which helped me at the time, and still do, to keep my feet on the ground.

When I was serving as locum tenens at Newarthill, I was conducting the annual flower service and although I was not quite daft enough as to imagine that I had the whole large congregation of adults and children in the palm of my hand, I did think that things were going along quite successfully. Then we came to the scheduled short address. I had barely got out the first two sentences when a little boy in the gathering yelled at the top of his voice, "Mammy, I want to go home now!"

Once the uproar (of laughter) had subsided, during which the little lad and his poor shamestricken mother departed the scene, I continued with the address but it was a bit much for a raw 23-year-old to contend with and I was relieved to get to the end of the service without further interruption.

I was able to cope years later when, as I stood at the church door after morning service in High Carntyne, thinking to myself that the service had gone quite well, one of the exiting congregation, grasped my hand and said, "Great stuff! If I'd known you were going to be so good today, I'd have brought my wife."

I was not quite sure, all the same, just how to take that remark. I was never left in any doubt, however, as to how my Newmilns session clerk had judged my Sunday services. Ernest Ling took the preaching part of worship very seriously and used to sit with an open notebook, taking copious notes as I preached, in his seat in the side gallery directly over-looking the pulpit. That in itself was disconcerting enough. But what was even worse for a young minister in his first charge was the habit Mr. Ling had of calling on me on a Monday morning if he had disapproved of anything I had said in the course of Sunday's preaching.

If the sermons passed muster so far as he was concerned, he did not come near. But I soon came to realise that, when he appeared at the manse door on a Monday morning, it meant that I was in disfavour for some lack of soundness in doctrine or some unwise statement.

It was rather unnerving for me at that stage in my ministry, and my lack of experience plus my youthful naivety meant that I was ill-equipped to handle the situation. I simply put up with it, unlike my predecessor who, faced with a similar situation, just told Ernest not to waste the time of both of them by calling in to dissect the previous day's preaching material.

Ernest Ling's attempt to have me conform in my preaching to what he saw as ideal in style and context struck me as unhelpful and did nothing to influence me to make sure I said only the kind of things that would please him.

I was more receptive to the much more kindly and gentler word of criticism spoken in my ear one Sunday night by John Miller, session clerk of Newarthill, part-way through my locumship there. "I like your preaching very much—we all do—but you are always trying to 'make' Christians. Don't forget that the majority of your congregation are Christians already and they, too, need to be catered for."

That wise and charitable comment was a

timely one and I think it was of benefit to my preaching and to the congregations who then and in the ensuing years had to listen to it. If nothing else, it caused my sermons to have a wider range of subject matter.

Sermons have always been a favourite focus of comment and the butt of innumerable jokes. It is quite difficult often to determine whether a particular sermon-based anecdote is completely apocryphal or rooted in original fact.

There is, for instance, that much quoted tale of the vacancy committee who had been out 'hearing' one of the candidates for their church. At the meeting they held on their return to assess the preacher, one member of the committee opened—and virtually closed—the proceedings by declaring: "He won't do. For one thing, he *read* his sermon, for another thing, he didn't read it well, and for a third thing, it wasn't worth reading."

One can well imagine this being an actual occurrence. Similarly with the following tale. A minister was being lavishly praised by a female parishioner for what she averred was the outstanding quality of his sermons.

"Your Sermons are absolutely marvellous," she declared.

"Oh, no," he protested, "They're not as good as all that."

"Oh, yes, they are," she insisted. "In fact they are so good you ought to have them published."

"Now, now," he again protested modestly, "That *is* going too far. They are not up to that standard."

"Oh, they are," she persisted. "They really should be in print."

"Well," he said, hoping to satisfy her, "Perhaps they will be published posthumously."

"The sooner the better!" she cried. "The sooner the better!"

Taken too literally, that might have caused the minister some little discomfiture; and I can remember more than one instance in my own experience which had that sort of effect.

One Sunday morning, in my student days, after conducting the service in a church in Motherwell, my home town, I was warmly complimented by one of the senior office-bearers who said, with obvious sincerity, "That was the finest sermon I have ever heard."

I was pleased, elated and, I am afraid, not a little conceited about my preaching ability because of that remark. I had, however, to wait only until the following Sunday to be brought back to earth with a thud.

I was taking the service in the same church and the office-bearer who had praised me so warmly the previous week was again in his place in the very front pew. I was not long into my sermon when I observed that he had fallen asleep. His head had dropped forward on to his chest, his eyes were firmly closed and, the very second my eyes lighted upon him, I saw his wife take her elbow and give him an almighty dig in the ribs. This brought his head up with a jerk and, poor soul, he glanced frantically all around, clearly most embarrassed.

He settled down to listen to the sermon, his eyes fixed intently on me. But a minute or two later the process was gone through all over again; and was repeated another twice before the sermon came to an end.

"So much for his 'marvellous' verdict on last

week's sermon," I thought ruefully to myself, "He was probably just being kind."

He was in a hurry to see me once the service was concluded, accompanied by his wife, to apologise profusely and to explain that he had been on night-shift, had come on to church without any sleep and the warm atmosphere of the church had made it too difficult for him to keep awake. Ah, well, all very true, no doubt, but the lesson had been learnt anyway and the balloon of my conceit well and truly deflated.

That same lesson advising me to be humble so far as my preaching was concerned was reinforced one day during my early years in Glasgow. I had a pulpit exchange one Sunday with an elderly minister in my area of the city—a lovable man but, I suspected, probably a little bit dull in the pulpit. When the service was over, the elders assembled in the vestry, as was their custom, to thank the visitor.

Their spokesman said, "Thank you for coming, Mr. Martin, we have greatly enjoyed your conduct of the service. I think these exchange services are a great idea. They help you to appreciate your own man all the more."

The preacher has to try not to be too much affected by any comments he may hear—or over-hear—about his sermons. His great privilege is to proclaim the Good News, the Gospel, the best of all good news and he must seek to do so in season and out of season to the best of his ability.

Taken seriously, the making and preaching of sermons is a most exacting task. Not that this is universally recognised.

One Saturday morning I was being delivered back to the manse after a funeral and, in the course of conversation, the driver of the car said, "Is that you finished for the day? Or do you have some other work to do?"

"For one thing," I replied, "I will have to finish writing my sermons for tomorrow."

In genuine astonishment, he said to me, "Do you mean to say you make them up yourself? I always thought ministers got their sermons out of books."

He is by no means alone in so thinking; and it is true that a few preachers have been known to obtain their sermons at second hand, either on an occasional or a more regular basis. Sometimes this has been a matter of blatant plagiarism.

My professor of Practical Training at Divinity College—that is, to do with preaching, conduct of church service and the like—was himself a very distinguished preacher with a number of volumes of published sermons to his name, A. J. Gossip. One day in urging us always to create our own sermon material and warning us against the temptation to plagiarism, he told us of an experience of his own.

Holidaying in Ireland one summer, he went to the local Presbyterian church on the Sunday morning. To his surprise but not to his delight, he heard the minister deliver one of Gossip's own published sermons, obviously 'lifted' verbatim from the book. At the close of the service Gossip made a point of speaking with the minister.

After shaking hands and thanking him for the worship, Gossip went on, "I liked your sermon but I must confess that I really liked it better when I preached it myself."

"Oh," beamed the minister, "Do you use the same book as I do?"

The preacher, if he has any wisdom at all, will make as full use as possible of other peoples' researches, scholarship, comments and learning about the scriptures; but, if it is to be truly effective, the message he preaches and delivers must in its finished form be his own. This will undoubtedly mean a lot of hard work and that itself may well be a surprise to many church members. Not a few of them seem to think that his Sunday sermons must come easily to the man of the cloth, effortlessly put together in a spare moment or two.

I have been asked many times, as I suppose

most ministers have, "How long does it take you to write a sermon?" But that is a difficult question to answer precisely. In a very real sense one might reply, "The preparation of each sermon has taken me the major part of my life." That would be true but would sound a bit pompous; and in any case that is not the answer the questioner is after. He wants to know how many hours are spent at the study desk over any particular sermon; and it is next to impossible to give an exact figure.

Some weeks there is little or no difficulty in choosing text and theme—the subject is just clamouring to be pursued—and often, when that is the case, thoughts and words will come swiftly and fluently to be set down on the paper. In other weeks, hours may be spent before even a beginning is made and the finished product may well be the result of much hard labour. That man was not far off the mark who said that "a good sermon was usually ten per cent inspiration and ninety per cent perspiration."

Hard labour but in a good cause. In the *best* of causes, indeed, for the preacher's message may lead, under God, to the assistance, even to the salvation, of one or more of his hearers.

chapter ten

office-bearers meetings

One area where the whole is not necessarily—
and perhaps not often—simply the sum of its parts is
that of church office-bearers. All through my ministry
I had—with very few exceptions—exceedingly cor-
dial relationships with all my office-bearers, elders
and managers alike. In most cases they were both
friendly and supportive as individuals; but sometimes
I found them rather different when they were acting as
an elected group, the kirk session or the management
committee or the congregational board.

My first, and somewhat shattering, experience
of this was in my first months at Newmilns West.
Being of the former United Presbyterian tradition,
they operated with a management committee
alongside the kirk session; and, as frequently was the
case with the U.P. constitution, the session and the
managers were completely separate bodies, with no
one, not even the minister, a member of both and each
doing its own thing without reference to the other.
The remit of the kirk session was the 'spiritual' side of
the congregation while the managers had to do with
the 'material'. Good friends with one another as they
might be, and usually were, as individual members of
the congregation, so far as their functions as elders

and as managers were concerned, it was mostly a case of "never the twain shall meet".

This system of operation might seem to contain the seeds of potential trouble and so it did, as was discovered during the vacancy shortly before my arrival. The church officer died suddenly and, in due course, the kirk session decided to insert an advertisement in the local paper, it being their responsibility to appoint a replacement. To their horror, and to the embarrassment of the whole congregation, the advertisement appeared almost side by side with a similar one which had been inserted by the management committee who had decided that they would see about filling the vacancy.

This episode created a good deal of annoyance among those Newmilns people who were part of the West Church and a good deal of hilarity among those who were not; and the wounds were still painful when I came upon the scene. When I learned about it, as I did very quickly, I felt that some measure of liaison between the two bodies would surely have prevented such an unnecessary debacle. As a result when, soon afterwards, we decided to appoint some new elders and those elected included a few from the management committee, I thought I had found a ready-made safeguard against anything similar ever happening again which everyone was sure to approve and probably applaud.

I called a meeting of elders and managers together and put my proposal. "I know of the church officer business during the vacancy," I began, "and of the great distress it caused. It seems clear that it all could have been avoided if there were some members common to both session and management. Soon we are to admit some of the managers to the kirk session.

I suggest that two of these should retain membership of the management committee as well, which would ensure that the two bodies could not again unknowingly take action on the same job."

Having said my piece, I sat back rather smugly, waiting to be clapped on the back. In fact, I was lucky I did not get beaten about the head.

One of the senior elders rose to his feet in horrified anger. "The kirk session and the managers have always been completely separate in personnel. Does Mr. Martin think that he can come here and after six months dare to change what we've been doing for 173 years? It's absolute nonsense!"

And so my marvellous idea for improvement was slain at birth and my process of learning of the ways of office-bearers in committee was begun. It was

an elder who shot down my suggestion on that occasion, although by far the majority present, elders and managers alike, thought as he did. But I discovered that the managers, too, nice people individually where I was concerned, could be very 'cussed' as a body.

My stipend was £370 a year which was £10 above the then obligatory minimum. After some time I discovered that the Ferguson Bequest paid a supplement of £35 to ministers in Ayrshire who were receiving only the minimum stipend. Since I had always been good at arithmetic, I realised that if my stipend were dropped to £360 and I then applied as a minimum stipend man to the Ferguson Bequest, the nett result would be that I would gain £25 and the congregation funds would gain £10.

I put this suggestion forward to the managers, expecting that they would be as delighted as I to adopt it. No such luck!

"We've always prided ourselves on paying our minister above the minimum," was the verdict delivered to me, "and we intend to keep it that way."

So that was that. And that was how it remained. All my eight years in Newmilns I was paid £10 above the minimum rate and consequently never qualified for the Ferguson Bequest, which would have been a godsend to us in those impecunious days.

My Newmilns financial court was not alone in my experience in its adoption of what seemed to me— admittedly an interested party—a suspect logic in matters monetary. There was an occasion in High Carntyne when, after I had been away for two weeks on holiday, my then assistant told me that during my absence he had had to use his car unexpectedly often for pastoral calls. He asked if I would have any objections to his tendering a request to the finance committee for £5 to cover the extra outlay on petrol.

I concurred and his request was duly tendered. After deliberating on it, the finance committee intimated to me that they considered the assistant had a legitimate claim for reimbursement of the £5. But, since he was out of pocket in the first instance through using petrol which I would have been using had I been at home, they considered that it was I who ought to do the reimbursing. Believe it or not—and it took me some time to realise they were serious—that was their final decision.

I suppose I ought not to have been all that surprised at what still strikes me as peculiar meanness as well as peculiar logic. I had had experience of it at the very beginning of my ministry in High Carntyne.

I was inducted to High Carntyne on the 20th January 1954 and my stipend was £700 per annum. At the end of the month I received a cheque from the Treasurer for £19-8-10, with an enclosed statement from him to the effect that this represented the payment due to me of 1/3 of a month's stipend. Being remarkably knowledgable about some things, I was aware that January contained 31 days and that I, therefore, had worked 12/31 of the month not 1/3 and should therefore have been paid £22-11-7.

I made no mention of this, either at the time or later, although in those days £3 was a not insubstantial sum to us. But I certainly noticed what was at best ungenerous thoughtlessness and at worst penny-pinching meanness. The disappointment I felt over this was somehow accentuated shortly afterwards when the treasurer of Newmilns West dealt in such a different way with a financial adjustment to me.

In those days the minimum stipend figure was

always fixed retrospectively, once the Edinburgh committee knew how much money was available. When there was an increase, this meant a very welcome back payment in a lump sum for the ministers who were on the minimum or, as I was, just above it. Some time after my arrival in High Carntyne the minimum stipend for 1953 was fixed at an increase of £35 over 1952.

This meant that I was due a back payment from Newmilns West which duly arrived and very soon. To my surprise it was a payment not only for the past year but also for a month, a full month, of the current year, rounded up to £3. This latter was not a large amount but that it should have been given— especially when thought of it had not even entered my head—touched me deeply.

My earlier years in High Carntyne were fraught with instances of seeming parsimony on the part of the financial court not only with regard to me but in other fields, too. As time went by (and as new personnel took over?) their attitude changed considerably for the better. I rather think that what was, sometimes at least, the cheeseparing policy of the earlier days may have been a direct legacy from the pioneering times of the 1930's when the congregation, founded bravely in the heart of a brand new housing scheme, had to treasure every penny, as it built itself up from its opening day when there was a congregation of some twenty souls and an offering of £1-13-9.

In any event, all through there was good fellowship—and a lot of good fun. Too much at times for at least one of my elders. At the kirk session meeting he felt constrained to rise in rebuke, after I had made some kind of joke. "I want to object to the levity and laughter that we have in these meetings at times. The

kirk session is no place for that kind of thing. It's for
serious business and not for making jokes."

Fortunately, few, if any, of the elders thought
as he did and the fun which we often had continued—
without, I think, any detriment to the serious business.

In my experience church office-bearers in their
official grouping, be it kirk session or management
committee or congregational board, could be exas-
perating and even infuriating; but they could be, and
often were, quite marvellous. I look back with pleasure, for instance, on more than one occasion when
they showed themselves in that light with regard to
me personally.

The High Carntyne kirk session, for instance,
organised a most memorable night of celebration of
the semi-jubilee of my ordination to the ministry
(with the considerable aid of my then assistant, David
Hamilton). Somehow they managed, with my wife's
connivance, to arrange it without my knowing anything at all about it except that there was to be a social
evening in the church on my anniversary evening.

I fondly imagined that the secrecy was so that
the identity of the artistes performing at the social
evening might provide me with a pleasant surprise.
On that basis I accepted without demur and without
suspicion the request of the convener of the social
committee, Jimmy Penman, that I should keep out of
sight and sound in the vestry, with him for company,
until we heard the opening hymn.

When the hymn ended, he led me into the
church. I shall never forget the reception I then
received or the programme that followed. What had
been planned was a 'This is Your Life' presentation
with many of my friends from the past and the present

smuggled secretly into the premises while I was safely out of the way in the vestry. And the church itself was packed with members of the congregation who rose, on my entry, to give me an ovation that seemed to me in my astonished and emotional state to go on and on and on.

That sort of experience went a long way to compensate for the disappointments and discouragements sometimes suffered in the regular meetings of the office-bearers; and afforded another instance of the value of being able to count one's blessings.

chapter eleven

some people in my ministry

By the nature of the case my work as a minister has revolved round people and they have presented a tremendous variety. Most have been very likeable although a few have been quite the reverse. I would like to tell you about a few of those who come most readily to mind.

Connie had many strange facets—not only in my judgment but also in that of nearly everyone who knew her.

As it happened, she was one of the first persons I visited after my induction to High Carntyne. I had been given a 'sick list' by the minister who had been acting as locum tenens during the vacancy. I made it my business to go round all of them in the first week. I discovered to my astonishment that, apart from one who had died, every one of those ill people was now fully recovered. The list was so out of date that in spite of myself I began to entertain just the very faintest suspicion that perhaps the locum had not been doing any sick visiting in recent times.

Be that as it may, as a consequence of that out-of-date sick-visiting list, Connie was one of the first High Carntyne members I got to know. But ours was a rather chequered relationship. I fell out of her favour early on and never was able to effect much improvement in that regard—rather the reverse if the truth be told.

My first misdemeanour so far as she was concerned was my failure to visit her living-room after it suffered damage by fire. I was genuinely sorry and sympathetic, as we all were, when I heard about the fire in her house and the damage it had caused and I said so to her when I saw her a day or two afterwards. But I did not realise until considerably later that it was a source of much annoyance to her that I was content with that and did not go to the house to inspect the damage for myself and offer my commiserations on the spot.

Worse to come. I had managed to repair fairly effectively the breach between us when I fell foul of her again. We had given the local health service department the use of our halls for pre-natal and post-natal clinics, until they were able to find suitable premises of their own. This arrangement continued for a year or two and, since we received quite generous financial donations as compensation for the inconvenience and expenses incurred, the church funds were that much healthier during that period.

One day Connie stopped me on the street, all excitement, "I have just had it on good authority that the clinic people are dissatisfied with the level of heating in our hall and are negotiating to buy premises of their own in the parish. Now, their donations are a valuable source of income for the church and I would advise you to get in touch with the authorities at once. Assure them that you will step up the heating and persuade them there is no need for them to seek other premises."

I thanked her for her concern but assured her that the heating problem had already been attended to

and that, in any case, I was aware that it had always been the intention of the health authorities to acquire their own clinic premises once something suitable came on the market.

"No, no," she insisted, "I am sure that if you promise them all will be well with the heating, then they will be only too pleased to stay where they are."

Shortly afterwards, the health authorities intimated that they now had their own premises for the clinic, would be moving there in two months time and thanked us most warmly for our hospitality during the waiting period. Connie was convinced, and remained so ever afterwards, that their removal was entirely the result of my failure to act upon her advice. I had insulted her and at the same time allowed the church to lose revenue which had been of considerable assistance to it.

She never forgave me for what she regarded as a wilful neglect of a lifeline which she had offered to me. And this despite the fact that there was nothing that could have been done either by me or by anyone else that would have changed things.

As a direct result of her umbrage over this incident, Connie transferred her membership to a neighbouring church. Her husband, however, who had long learned to live with her idiosyncrasies, refused point blank to do the same insisting that he "liked and admired" me. We had, therefore, the potentially embarrassing situation of my continuing to be the minister of a man whose wife had sought pastures elsewhere because, so far as she was concerned, I had shown myself to be unsatisfactory.

Since Alex, her husband, fell ill not long afterwards, I had occasion to visit him regularly over a lengthy period. With someone other than Connie, the previous history between us could have made my house-visiting very awkward. But she was not in the least embarrassed—after all, she 'knew' she was in the right—and I was determined not to be. I refused even to let myself become too ruffled by the way in which she found occasion in the course of nearly ever visit to remind me of how my spurning of her advice had cost the church a worthwhile source of income.

Connie was a kenspeckle figure in the parish and it was the general opinion that her well known eccentricities of thought and judgment were the result of an irrational element embedded in her make up. I am sure there was much truth in that opinion. I do not think she was ever intentionally malicious, which is more than I would care to say for *Jimmy*.

Jimmy was a member of the kirk session and had been a member of the vacancy committee which had presented me to the congregation as their sole nominee to be their new minister. We seemed—or so I thought—to get along all right at first, but gradually, and more frequently, he began to oppose me and my ideas at the kirk session meetings. I became increasingly concerned about this because his obstructionist attitude did not seem to me to help the church business which was our responsibility or the atmosphere of Christian fellowship which I desired for our meetings.

There came one session meeting when he proved particularly troublesome to me in the chair and eventually I said to him, "You and I are not seeing eye-to-eye about a number of things. Perhaps we might come to a better understanding if we have some private conversation in the vestry once this meeting is concluded."

And so I sat down with him in the vestry a little bit later. "Jimmy," I said, "You seem nowadays to make difficulties with practically everything I bring up in the session. Where do you think I am going wrong?"

"Everywhere," was his immediate reply. "The truth is that I just don't like you and the way you do your work. You're just not the man for High Carntyne."

"What has changed your mind about me?" I asked. "You were a member of the vacancy committee and the choice of me was unanimous."

"Oh, I just went with the rest to make it look better. I was never in favour of you coming here. You are far too *evangelical* for my liking."

My attempt at reconciliation having proved a

dismal failure, except that I now knew I had not been imagining his animosity, Jimmy became more than ever a thorn in my flesh—and in the flesh of many others, too. I kept hoping he would have a change of heart but I suppose that the end of his High Carntyne association, when it came, was more or less inevitable.

That end, as it happened, was not through any disagreement or confrontation with me. One night at the congregational board meeting, Jimmy was taken severely to task by the Clerk, Jack Forbes, because he had acted and spoken very much out of turn at the annual business meeting of the congregation which had taken place recently. When the next year's business meeting approached, he was warned that he must observe the proprieties.

Despite the warning, Jimmy again insisted on speaking out of turn, and the matter was raised at the next board meeting. As soon as the subject was mentioned, Jimmy rose to his feet and marched out in high dudgeon. In his absence it was moved, seconded and carried unanimously that the board administer a reprimand to Jimmy.

It was then I made my big mistake. I was at that time even more naive, not to say positively stupid, than I sometimes showed myself to be in my more experienced years. I liked always to have everything tidily tied up, which was a pity. If I had kept my mouth shut at that precise moment, it may be that that would have been the end of the matter and I would not have had the embarrassment and the discomfort of standing for nearly an hour in the rain on Jimmy's doorstep.

But speak I did. "How is the reprimand to be conveyed to Jimmy?" I asked. "I suppose the clerk will send him a letter?"

One of the members jumped to his feet, and said with emotion, "This is a very serious matter and must be handled as delicately as possible. A letter won't do. I move that the minister should call on Jimmy with our decision and try to get him to see how wrong he was."

Everyone, minister excepted, thought this was a great idea—especially the clerk—and the minister had not the gumption to decline the honour, so abruptly thrust upon him. And so one wet night that same week I presented myself at Jimmy's door and rang the bell.

When he opened the door and saw who was there, he made no move to admit me. "May I come in, Jimmy?" I asked. "I would like to have a talk with you."

"If you're to bring me a reprimand," he replied (so much for the confidentiality of the meeting), "you're not getting through this door."

And for fifty-five minutes, with Jimmy in the dry on the inside of the threshold and me in the wet on the outside, I tried my best to build bridges and persuade him to see some things differently, but all to no avail. He never again entered the church, even though I made it plain when I left him that the door would always be open.

I did come into contact with him on two later occasions, however. The first was when he was a mourner at a funeral I was conducting.

"Hallo, Jimmy,' I said. "How are you keeping?"

"My health," he replied frostily, "is no business of yours."

His health, however, did become my business in an indirect fashion some years later when he was

admitted as a patient to the little local hospital to
which I acted as chaplain. I thought at first his attitude
to me had thawed somewhat with the passing of time.
As I made my week-day tour of the wards in which I
had a brief word with each patient, Jimmy answered
me pleasantly enough when I came to him.

But I discovered on his first Sunday that little
had really changed. I had a brief church service every
Sunday afternoon to which all the patients were invited. My helpers and I used to go round the wards and
personally invite those mobile enough to attend. On
this first Sunday I made a point of going myself to
Jimmy.

"We have a short service, Jimmy, starting in a
few minutes time. Would you like to come?"

"No, thanks," he said, which was a disappointment but no surprise. As I left the ward, I heard
him say to the man sitting next to him, "I'm not going
to his service. I don't believe in any of that bloody
nonsense."

I had another Jimmy who caused me a few
headaches, or *James* to be more precise. He presented
himself at my vestry hour one Monday night and
declared his wish to transfer his membership to High
Carntyne. He explained that he worked every Sunday
morning, his present church no longer held an evening service and since we were the only church in the
area that held a regular Sunday evening service, he
wished to come to us.

For years he and I had a very warm and
friendly relationship, but that relationship began to
deteriorate when the kirk session decided to cut out
some of the evening services. At the time James joined
us we had evening services every Sunday of the year
except in the Glasgow holiday period of July. It was

when the kirk session decided to extend that evening close-down period for an additional two months, that James began to complain more and more persistently to me about the absence of the evening service on so many Sundays of the year, sweeping aside my plea that it was the kirk session and not I who had made the decision.

What made the situation ironic and, to me, extremely disappointing so far as James was concerned was that by this time he had retired and was completely free to attend morning worship if he chose. But he did not choose. The church was too crowded in the morning, he protested, and not nearly so much to his liking as the much less well attended evening service. It was difficult to feel total sympathy for his complaint that he was being deprived the opportunity of attending worship during the three summer months when he could perfectly well have come to church on the Sunday mornings.

His boiling point was reached over the kirk session's refusal to have an evening service on Easter Sunday. I persuaded the kirk session to institute an annual dawn service on Easter day in addition to our regular 11 a.m. service. In view of our having the extra early service—usually somewhere around 5 a.m.—the kirk session decided it would be wise to dispense with the evening service.

James was furious that we should fail to have an evening service on the most important day in the Christian year. He blamed me bitterly for this omission, and, try as I might, I was unable to effect a reconciliation with him. In the end he stormed out of the annual congregational meeting, flinging down his letter of resignation as he went, after making a vehement denunciation of the minister's culpability in allowing so many Sunday evenings in the year to be without an evening service.

Sadly, he did not associate himself with another congregation (there were, of course, none in the vicinity with a regular evening service) and so far as I know never went to another church service.

People like Connie and Jimmy and James were very much in the minority in my ministry. I would not dare to say that there were no other odd or difficult or awkward customers amongst the people I came across in my churches but by far the majority were likeable, pleasant, helpful and sensible, and more than a few were saintly.

Mary Brown certainly belonged to the latter category. All the 34 years I was her minister she spent herself selflessly in the service of others and I know that that was also the pattern of all her earlier life. Remaining unmarried, she tended her parents—aged by the time I came on the scene—with an indefatigable love. Totally uncomplaining it was, too, and with never a hint of the self-pity that would surely have been most excusable in view of the difficulties she often encountered with a rather cross-grained father much given to an over-indulgence in alcoholic beverages.

Even when she herself moved into the octogenarian grouping, her active concern for others refused to diminish. This was made very plain to me when she had a spell in hospital and I paid a call on her shortly after her discharge. I discovered that she was out paying a sick visit to a friend who was in my opinion in much better physical shape than Mary was at that particular time.

Mary was one of the jewels in High Carntyne's

crown of caring people, and there were others of similar stamp, not just 'do-gooders' of that insensitive type who are much maligned and who sometimes give the church a bad name. I never cease to thank God for the Marys of my ministry—in Newarthill, in Newmilns, in Carntyne, in Airdrie and in Wishaw.

No sooner have I written that sentence than a mass of faces swim into my vision from the past, the Marys of my ministry, although they had a multitude of different names. Margaret was one who, like Mary, humbled and inspired me all at once. In High Carntyne we were faced one year with expenditure of £60,000 for urgent repairs to our halls and had invited each of our members to bring as generous a contribution as they could to me in the vestry on a given day.

Margaret came along with a donation much larger than the average and much more than I considered she could afford to give.

"This is exceedingly generous of you, Margaret," I said, "But I really think you should take some of it back. I am sure we will get our required total in the end and I don't want you to be leaving yourself short."

"Dr. Martin," she said quietly, "I *want* to give this amount. Would you try to deprive me of the joy of giving it to my Saviour's church?"

Times without number I have been made to marvel at the devotion shown by my people. Occasionally, however, devotion was not matched with sensitivity and sometimes this had disastrous results.

Ernest Ling was an example. He was of fervent evangelical zeal, but the very ferocity of his zeal sometimes hindered the cause he was most anxious to promote. This was seen, for example, in his involvement with the Bible study evening I started in Newmilns. It was a very ordinary type of Bible study meeting. I presided and gave a fairly brief exposition of the Bible passage which I had selected for the evening, after which I threw open the meeting for general comment and discussion.

For the first month, Ernest, to his expressed deep regret, was unable to attend owing to previous commitments of one kind and another. During this initial period, the group grew and grew in numbers until at the end of the first month there were no less than thirty people attending, most of whom were chipping in their contributions to the discussions.

Then Ernest Ling came on the scene, full of enthusiasm and also of Biblical knowledge and understanding which he was determined to thrust upon the meeting. Looking back I realise only too well that my inexperience and naivety rendered me quite unfitted to deal with him properly in that context.

I allowed him to speak far too often and far too long. Increasingly few of the other group members were able or willing to make a contribution to the discussions. After several weeks of this, the numbers began a steady decline which no efforts of mine or Ernest's were able to arrest. When the night arrived that only Ernest Ling and James Martin turned up, I realised that facts had to be faced and the Bible study ceased to be.

Most of the people I encountered during my years of ministry are, thank God, the objects of much fond memory on my part. Many have been generous and gracious enough to express gratitude for help and even inspiration they claimed to have received from me. Such things make happy and enduring memories but I for my part am much more in debt to those many men and women—and boys and girls, too—who have been of help and inspiration to me.

Among these Bill McColl is in the forefront.

When I went to Newmilns West, Willie, as everyone then knew him, was a youth with talent for music. When I started up a youth fellowship his name was suggested to me as a likely pianist and I went off without delay to ask him if he would give me his assistance.

That was the beginning of a rich and enriching friendship which remains strong today even though his home has been in Canada for the past thirty-five years. Although he was several years my junior, Willie and I soon established a remarkable rapport. One manner in which this found expression was in what soon became regular Sunday evening sessions round the manse fire at the close of the youth fellowship meeting. Sunday after Sunday Willie and one or two others would come with me up to the manse when the meeting was over. Marion, my wife, would have the fire banked up high in the grate, she would make tea and an enormous mound of toast; and we would talk and talk until the large blazing fire had become no more than a residue of grey ash.

In those Sunday evening sessions many deep questions were asked and for me at least the beginnings of some answers were found. If these embryonic answers matured in my mind into something that was of help to others as well as myself in later years, that was due in no small measure to Willie McColl and many others of those people I was involved with in my ministry. I thank God for them.

chapter twelve

shepherd of the sheep

Pastoral visitation is one of my richest seams of memory lore as I look back on my ministerial years. Despite the fact that, like every other minister, I had my share of difficult visits, depressing visits, unproductive visits, sad visits, I recall a mass of visits whose very memory even now entertains, enriches and inspires me.

I have never attempted to make an accurate accounting of the number of pastoral visits paid in the course of my ministry but I know they numbered many thousands and by far the majority I can look back on with great pleasure. This might seem a little surprising when I have to admit that at least the initial visit to any house was invariably for me an occasion of considerable stress and strain.

Although I am naturally a gregarious person— and I thank God for that—I have also a basic shyness which makes my first approach to any person or group of persons a rather painful process for me. It is almost like a visit to the dentist, when any good excuse for postponement is warmly welcomed.

My innate feelings of diffidence and apprehension were accentuated rather than eased by my experience the first evening I launched out into pastoral visitation on my own in Newmilns. I had a few calls to make in the town's Riverbank Street and was totally unaware that entrance to the houses in that street was quite different from anything I had previously encountered.

The street presented an attractive and orderly appearance with its row of neat storm doors abutting the pavement, all firmly shut. Consulting the numbers on my list, I presented myself before the first of my doors and knocked. My knock was, I felt, a bit timid, indicative of my inner desire to turn and flee; and I was not greatly surprised that it failed to elicit a response. So I knocked again, this time more firmly, but still there was no answer. Hope was beginning to rise that somehow there was no one at home but conscience decreed that I make one further attempt before giving up. So I beat a thunderous tattoo on the door just as a man walked past.

"My son," he said kindly, "You'll hammer there all night without getting a reply. That's the door into the passage *between* the houses. Just open it and go in, and you'll find the house door inside." And so I did.

Having learned from my mistake, I was certainly not going to make a fool of myself a second time. And so when I came to the second number on my list, a little further along the street, I remembered what to do. Without any vain beating upon the door, I simply turned the handle and plunged through—to find myself in the living room of the house I had come to visit. Fortunately, all the occupants were fully dressed and were neither drinking nor gambling. But it was a rather red-faced young minister who made his explanations and his introductions.

That experience did nothing to ease the diffidence and nervousness I had always felt in going to visit anyone for the first time. I had to learn to control my shyness and to 'press on regardless', but it remained with me even after more than forty ministerial years of which a considerable part was spent knocking on unfamiliar doors.

Despite all this, my pastoral visitation has left me with many marvellous memories of many marvellous people. Not a few of them were sermons in themselves and more eloquent ones than any I preached from the pulpit.

Old Mrs. McIntosh in Newmilns High Street was one of these. When I went to Newmilns, she had already been widowed for thirty years and for most of these years she had been virtually a prisoner—through age and infirmity—in her attic dwelling at the top of a flight of wooden stairs. She was never out except for those happy but infrequent occasions when she permitted friends to carry her downstairs for an outing in their car.

I visited her often and found her irrepressibly joyful at all times. Her flow of conversation never ceased and her memory was able to reach far back in a way that was full of interest to her young minister. On one occasion at least it was also a bit disconcerting.

One afternoon, in the course of our conversation, she started to speak of her memories of David Livingstone and his great missionary explorations in Africa. I found it fascinating, but I did not quite know how to take it when she said, "What a great time that was when Livingstone came back to Scotland after his great journey across Africa. You'll mind it fine?"

Despite her apparent assumption that I was capable of personal recollection stretching back as far as her ninety-year life span took her, I found her vivid personal reminiscences—not only of Livingstone's triumphal return home but also of many another historic occasion—exhilarating and inspiring as well as informative.

My most abiding memory of her, however, is of her serene Christian faith, uncluttered by doubt or uncertainty. How well I recall her saying to me, "People think I must be very lonely, living up here all by myself these many years. But they're wrong. I'm no' lonely at all. Because, you see. I'm never ma lane. The Maister's aye beside me."

It was a similar kind of absolute trust—that did my own faith a power of good—which I encountered in Mr. Munro, another old parishioner of mine in Newmilns. Well into his eighties, he had been bedridden for a considerable period of time. Week after week I used to call on him and our conversation always opened in the same way, "How are you today?" I would ask; and invariably he would reply, "I'm fine."

One afternoon when I entered his bedroom, his physical condition had noticeably deteriorated. But when I offered my usual, "How are you today?", he came back as always with "I'm fine." He must have noticed in my face the concern I was certainly feeling and he followed up by saying, with a radiant smile, "Don't be anxious for me. I have a great future ahead of me."

I had no doubt—as he had no doubt—that that was the case: and it was only a few hours later that he slipped into the great future awaiting him with God.

It was not only in Newmilns that I met faith that strengthened my own faith. I had many such encounters in Glasgow, too. I went one desperately wet and wild afternoon to make my regular call on a

man who had been a long time in hospital and who would, we both knew well, be there until he died.

As I went into his ward, with the rain sheeting down outside, I said to him, "This is a terrible day, isn't it?"

But I did not elicit the expected agreement. Quite the reverse, in fact, "No, no," he declared, "This is a good day. Every day is a good day, for the sun is always shining somewhere."

Isa Edgar was another of the many shining jewels in my pastoral visitation crown. Active in the church and a teacher in the Sunday School, she had been badly incapacitated by a severe stroke some months before I went to High Carntyne. She was then only in her mid-twenties.

When I first visited her, she could make no conversation and was able to walk only a very little and with extreme difficulty. She was much dependent on her mother, father and brother with whom she shared an upstairs flat. As time went by, she very gradually improved both in walking and in speaking, but only to a limited extent. She never regained the ability to walk freely and, while she eventually was able to move around considerably more than when I made her acquaintance, her mobility was always very slow, laborious and restricted.

Her speech never regained anything approaching fluency, although she improved enough to communicate clearly, even if slowly. She was never able to speak in sentences but her patient perseverance enabled her to conduct a halting kind of conversation mainly by means of single, independent words.

That was as far as her physical rehabilitation ever reached and all the 34 years that I was her minister, life was very difficult for her in many ways and was made ever so much more difficult by the deaths, one after the other, of her brother, her father and finally her mother. She continued to live on in the same house, on her own. I often used to wonder how she managed, but manage somehow she did.

I hope that my pastoral visits were of some assistance to her; they assuredly were to me. Although so much handicapped physically, she remained very

alert mentally and kept abreast of all the news in the
world, in the country and in the church through the
medium of television, radio and visitors.

The supremely marvellous thing about her
was her unconquerably joyous spirit. I never once
visited her—apart from her times of bereavement—
without being welcomed by a broad beaming smile.
And she always seemed to find enormous pleasure in
sharing vicariously the activities of her friends.
Nothing ever pleased me more after any of my television broadcasts than to have Isa welcome me on my
visit, see me seated securely and then, as she invariably did, burst into happy laughter and, pointing to
the television set, say, "Martin—telly—great."

When I remember people like Isa who were
able to count their blessings in the face of adversity, it
helps me to count my own; and not least among my
blessings have been the hundreds of such people to
whom I was privileged to be shepherd.

There were a great many other occasions
where the pastoral visit may not have been on such a
spiritual plane, but which nevertheless went a long
way to gladden my soul. For instance, I will never
forget going to visit old Mrs. Ferguson and being
highly entertained by her 80 year old husband in a
most unexpected way.

He was a very sprightly octogenarian and his
obvious pride in his sprightliness soon showed itself.
He was telling me about his working life as a joiner
and related an anecdote of how one day, as he was
walking along the street, he came upon a housewife
who had got herself trapped by the window frame on
her second floor tenement house. She had been sitting
on the window ledge, with her legs dangling inside,
in order to clean the window—a common practice

among Glasgow tenement dwellers—when the window cord had snapped. The heavy window had then plummetted down across her thighs and imprisoned her. She was quite unable to push it up and free herself.

As soon as he noticed the lady and her plight, Willie Ferguson called up, "Don't panic. I'll soon run up the stair and into the house and free you."

"You won't be able to get in," she said. "The front door is locked."

"I could see," said Willie, as he continued with his tale, "that she was in a panic and also in a good bit of pain. There was no time to lose. There wasn't time to go for a ladder or the fire brigade or anything like that, so I just dropped my tools and shinned up the drainpipe to the window and released her."

"That was terrific," I said in admiration. "You would be a good bit younger then, I suppose."

"Oh, aye," he replied, "I was only about sixty, but I could do it yet. I keep myself fit, you know. I do things like walking on my hands round the living room here. Here, I'll show you."

Without any more ado, he pushed around the furniture to create a clear space in the middle of the room. This done, he took off his jacket and hung it up. Next instant he sprang on to his hands as nimbly as you could imagine and proceeded to patter back and forward upside down in the most confident manner.

When he had finished his demonstration and resumed his seat, he asked with justifiable pride, "What do you think of that? Could you do it any better?"

"I think it was terrific," I replied, and I meant it. "As for doing any better, count me out. I never

could stand on my hands even when I was a school-
boy."

I suppose I could practically fill a whole book
with such tales culled from my pastoral visitation. I
will content myself, however, by signing off this chapter with two stories taken from opposite ends of the
age range I had to deal with.

One Monday evening I was paying a call on a
house whose ten-year-old son was a member of the
Junior Boys Brigade section which in those days was
known as the Life Boys. The boy was, I was aware, a
member of the Life Boys' football team and I also was
aware that they had been playing a match on the
previous Saturday morning. So, after a while, when I
brought the lad into the conversation, I enquired,
"How did you get on in last Saturday's match?"

"Oh," he said in disappointment, "we were
beaten 16–0. But," he added with deep feeling, "it was
the *goalie's* fault. He had a bad game."

I had known Mrs. Agnes Calvert well all my
years in High Carntyne and had shared with her
experiences of great joy and of great sorrow—in particular the marrage of her elder daughter on the one
hand, and, on the other hand, the funerals of her
husband and of her younger daughter. Our friendship
had been deep but for some time back Agnes had
been 'losing the place', becoming more and more for-
getful; and now, in her nineties, unable to live alone
and her married daughter in America, she was perma-
nently in hospital.

When I visited her, which I did frequently,
sometimes she knew me right away but more often
she failed to put a name to me before I gave her a hint.
As a result my opening remarks soon acquired a set
pattern.

I would say, "Well, Agnes, you're looking well today. Do you know who I am?"

On occasion she replied at once, "Of course, I know who you are. You're my minister. You're James Martin," and glowed with triumphant self-congratulation. On rather more occasions she would be likely to say, "Of course, I know you but I just can't place you;" but always in the end, with more or less assistance from me, she would arrive at my name.

There was one day, however, when our little game developed a surprising twist. "Well, then, Agnes," I had said, "do you know me today?"

This time she was rather more puzzled than she normally was. "No, I don't think I know you."

"Come on," I pleaded, "we've known each other a long time. Who am I?"

I could see her wrestling with the problem. Then suddenly her face cleared and she blurted out, "Are you my home help?"

With my well-known inability to be of much use in manual skills, these words soon became almost immortal in some High Carntyne circles.

chapter thirteen

manse and vestry callers

While the great majority of a minister's
pastoral contacts are the result of his calling at the
homes of his people, a considerable minority are the
result of someone calling at the manse or at the vestry.
During my years in Newmilns I had no specific time of
the week set apart for people to call on me. If they had
any matter to discuss, they simply looked in at the
manse in the hope of finding me in, or saw me in the
vestry after church service on Sunday, or telephoned
to make an appointment to see me at one or the other
of these locations.

This system worked, I think, quite well and
proved totally adequate for all the pastoral matters,
major and minor, that arose. When I moved to High
Carntyne and a parish population twice the size of the
whole town of Newmilns with its three Church of
Scotland charges, I inherited a weekly 'Vestry Hour'.
This meant that the minister was in attendance in his
vestry at a specified hour once a week to meet with
any and all who desired to see him.

In High Carntyne the vestry hour was a must.
The sheer volume of callers was such as could not have
been handled by the more casual Newmilns method.
Some nights my vestry 'hour' lasted for three hours,
with my devoted 'Minister's Man', Johnny Kincaid,

desperately trying—usually without success—to smuggle me in a cup of tea between callers. There were of course, still those who came direct to the manse, still those who laid hold of me on a Sunday, still those who made appointments; but without the weekly vestry hour it would have been extremely difficult to cope.

Many of the calls were concerned with fairly straightforward matters, like arranging marriages and baptisms, but a great many were to do with acute personal problems of one kind or another. In consequence, the bulk of the conversations that took place in my vestry or my manse between the caller and myself were, by the nature of the case, as private and as confidential as the confessional is meant to be; and therefore not for publication. But I am at liberty to say that they covered a very wide range of human experience.

I remember it being said to me, in rather pitying tones, "Ministers, of course, live sheltered lives. They can't possibly know what real life is like for they come into contact with so little of it." A few sessions eavesdropping on my vestry hour would surely have been sufficient to dispel that idea.

It was only in my later years in the ministry that there began to be talk of minister's 'burn-out' but the stresses and strains that lead to that kind of phenomenon were always there. In part these stresses and strains were the result of sharing the burdens brought by parishioners in need to manse or vestry.

Minister's wives could not always be protected from these stresses and strains even if they were not permitted to be privy to the details. What about manse wife's burn-out?

It may have had nothing at all to do with that

but I heard of one lady of the manse in Ayrshire who became rather eccentric. I did not know her personally but I am assured that the following tale of her treatment of one particular caller at the manse is absolutely accurate.

Answering the door bell one afternoon, she found a man standing on the step who enquired politely, "Could I see the minister, please?"

"You have come to the wrong door," was her reply. "People who come to see the minister go to the back door. You'll have to go round there."

A little puzzled but totally compliant, the caller made his way round to the back of the manse. There, sure enough, was a door and this door, too, had a bell. He rang the bell and in a few moments the door was opened by the minister's wife.

"Could I see the minister now, please?" he asked, just as politely as before.

"I am afraid you can't," she said. "The minister is not at home."

I do not think that any caller at my manse or my vestry ever received such scurvy treatment. But there were a number who perhaps should have done, the sponging con-men among them.

I was particularly plagued by the latter breed in our first High Carntyne manse—in Glasgow's Dennistoun area. It was located in a terrace most of whose houses were manses and which had, as a result, gained the popular appellation of Mount Zion. The con-men spongers regarded this as their happy hunting ground.

My first encounter with one of the fraternity was the evening of the very day we moved into the manse. Since we had two pre-school age children, after we had moved in our furniture and got the house to some semblance of order that day, my wife, Marion, went to Motherwell to spend the night with her mother who had had our two girls in her care during the removal operation. I stayed on in the manse and four of the office-bearers came along to 'help' me hang curtains and do other jobs (that means *they* did them with *minimal* assistance from me).

When the tasks were completed, I made a cup of tea and we were chatting over that when the door bell rang. I was all excited—my very first caller in our new manse and me not yet inducted to my new post. When I opened the door, I was met by a young couple, poorly dressed, and the woman was carrying a baby.

"Could you please give us some help?" the young man said. "Will you kindly give us a pound or two to tide us over until the morning? We've had nothing to eat all day, my wife's not well and the baby's hungry."

"You'd better come in," I said, "and explain your situation further."

Leaving my office-bearers undisturbed with their tea, I took my visitors into the kitchen and invited the young man to give me a fuller version of what struck me as a rather dubious tale.

"It's genuine, I swear it," he asserted. "I've a job waiting for me in Newcastle and I've got the fare to take us there. But that's all I've got and we couldn't get seats on the Newcastle bus today. We'll get on it tomorrow all right but we've nowhere to spend the night and no money to buy food. If you could help us out and lend us some money, I'll pay you back, I promise."

After a fairly lengthy dialogue, I eventually parted with a few pounds and off they went into the night. When I rejoined my office-bearers, Jack Forbes, the clerk to the congregational board, said, "I hope that wasn't somebody trying to 'make a touch' for some money. I am afraid you'll get a lot of that here."

Rather shamefacedly, I had to tell them the whole story. They shook their heads sadly and Jack said, sympathetically, "Put it down to experience but don't be so ready to part with your money the next time."

I never received a refund for my 'loan' but there was a sequel to that tale. Almost exactly a year later I answered a ring at the door bell and there before me was a young man accompanied by a young woman with a baby in her arms.

"We're in desperate need," he said, "Would you help us? I've a job to go to in Newcastle but we've missed the bus today and need some money to feed the baby and, what's more, my wife is ill."

I had recognised him the moment I opened the door. It was the same fellow who had been my first manse visitor a year ago. Here he was, with the identical story—but, as my memory clearly told me, not the identical 'wife'. It was a different woman than the one who had accompanied him the previous time.

Did he think that the passage of a year would have erased from my mind all memory of our previous meeting? Or—as seems to me more likely—had he been spinning this same yarn so often and to so many ministers that he had simply lost track of those who had already been duped by him.

As Jack Forbes forecast that first night in Broompark Drive, we had an endless procession of such would be beneficiaries calling at our door. Most had stories that ran in pretty similar grooves. A job waiting in Newcastle without the money to get there was a frequent feature. Other regular features were the ailing wife, the under-nourished child, the loss of their accommodation, the promise to pay the money back.

Some stories, however, were more ingenious and more elaborate. On one in particular I look back with unwilling admiration.

Having been taken in many times and never, to my knowledge, having had a single manse caller seeking money who was a genuine case, I had long since steeled my heart against all such doorstep appeals. Then one day, when the rain was pouring down, I answered the door to a man who looked far from well, and whose overcoat was absolutely sodden.

"You don't know me," he said, "but I am a former member of High Carntyne. I've just come from the church, where I got your address and I badly need your help."

"Oh, oh," I thought to myself. "Here we go again!" To him I said, "Where did you live when you were in Carntyne?"

Without hesitation he replied, "I lived in Haymarket Street near to Jack Wallace. He will remember me."

Jack Wallace was one of my senior elders who indeed lived in Haymarket Street. My suspicions were sufficiently allayed to persuade me that I could not in Christian charity keep the man standing at the door a minute longer in his soaking wet state. So I invited him in, took his wet coat and sat down with him in our drawing room. "Tell me more," I asked.

"I'm just back from Canada, where my family and I went from Carntyne before you came; and I collapsed on the street in Glasgow last week. I was taken to hospital and was discharged today; but my wallet is missing, someone must have stolen it when I was unconscious. The only person I could think of to turn to in emergency was the minister of my old church—and that's why I've come to you."

"I don't want to be uncaring," I said, "and you seem genuine enough, but I've been taken in so many times by hard luck stories and handed out money to so many undeserving cases that I was advised some time ago not to give or lend money to anyone without first checking his story. If you come back here at six o'clock that will give me time to do some checking, and if your story is verified, I'll lend you the money you want."

"All right," he replied, hesitantly. "I'll do that but can you suggest where I can spend the intervening time. I am soaked as you have seen, I have lost all my money, I'm only today discharged from hospital, and the rain is still pouring down. Here's a letter they gave me when I left so that I can get further medical attention right away." And he produced just such a letter from the hospital bearing that day's date.

I knew I had promised my office-bearers to part with no more money for a hard luck story before I had verified it. I knew that I was again letting my heart rule my head. But the man's story did seem to hang together; he did have knowledge of High Carntyne and at least some of its people; he *was* just out of hospital; and it *was* shockingly wet. And so I gave him a few pounds to see him sheltered and fed through the afternoon, arranging for him to return to the manse at 6 o'clock.

I never saw him—or my money—again.

After I reached the 'hardening of my heart' stage with the would be con-men at the manse door, a few of them responded by giving me some philosophy, often couched in lurid terms.

I ventured to question one of them a bit.

"You've come to me for money," I said. "But you admit that you have never met me, and have neither knowledge of nor connection with my church. Why, then, come to *me*?"

"Well," he said, apparently surprised that I had even thought it worthwhile to ask the question, "That's what you fellows are for, isn't it?"

I am not likely to forget his call, nor am I any more likely to lose my memory of the similar applicant who decided to record my rejection of his rather aggressive appeal for funds by supplying me with a few home truths as he saw them. When I told him, "I am sorry but I no longer give to people coming to the door like this," he at first refused point blank to believe me. When I repeated what I had said, he stared at me malevolently for a full minute, then walked away. But half way to the gate he stopped and turned to face me once more. Then he proceeded to tell me, at the top of his voice so that passersby within a radius of fifty yards could easily hear, and with a lurid expletive every second word, just how deficient my Christianity was.

When High Carntyne decided to sell the manse we first occupied because it was an old house constantly in need of repair and build a new one on a site close to the access road to Barlinnie Prison, we feared the high frequency of this type of caller at the manse door would increase. In the event the number decreased—no doubt because once discharged the former inmates of that institution had little desire to attempt to transact any kind of business too near to it.

We still had more than enough to satisfy us all the same. The usual kind of story was the need for money to take him or her home after having spent every penny on the journey to visit a relative in the

prison. In these instances the most common dramatis
personae were a woman and a baby.

There were variations. One Barlinnie caller I
particularly remember. It was a lovely spring morning
and I happened to be doing some weeding in my front
garden when I heard the garden gate click and found a
very pleasant and chatty man standing beside me.

After a fairly lengthy chat about the weather,
gardening and things in general, I finally asked him,
"Should I know you?"

"Not at all," he said. "I've just been released
from Barlinnie this morning."

"Oh, is that so?" I replied, and anxious not to
appear disinterested, I enquired, "What were you in
for?"

"Murder," he answered laconically. "I did my
wife in."

In addition to the various large categories of
callers at the manse of whom I have given a few
examples, we had a pretty large assortment of 'one-off'
types whose only apparent linking bond was that, in
some way each seemed to look to my manse as a haven
of refuge or, alternatively, an object on which to vent
their spite on the Church or on society.

Among those is to be numbered the teenaged
glue-sniffer who deliberately and with great violence
kicked in the glass panelling of our front door one
Saturday evening. My wife was left white and shaking
with shock. How much worse might her condition
have been if the incident had occurred some fifteen
minutes earlier, as I was only ten minutes returned
from a wedding reception.

Then there were the two young women who
rang my bell at 2 o'clock one very snowy Sunday
morning, having seen my light still on as I worked late

to complete the morning sermon. They were on their way home from a dance, they were out of cigarettes and they "just wondered if I could sell them or give them a few cigarettes." I had long ago forsaken 'the weed' and so was compelled—without feeling any pain, I confess—to send them back to their snowy journey with their nicotine hunger unsatisfied.

To our sorrow and to our annoyance there was a public house about fifty yards from the manse. The consequence was that frequently after the pub closed for the night we would have an inebriated gentleman at the door. Sometimes it was to beg assistance to get home. Sometimes it was to request a few roses from my front garden to take to his wife. Sometimes it was to raise a religious discussion. Sometimes it was just to pass the time of day—well, time of *night*, I suppose.

One evening, however, the inebriated late-night caller I had was seeking assistance not for himself but for another.

When I opened the door in response to the ringing of its bell, I saw before me the swaying figure of a man who seemed just able to remain erect without support.

"What can I do for you?" I asked as politely as my sinking heart would allow.

"Nothing for me," was the reply. "It's not me that's needing help. It's my mate. Will you give him a hurl hame in your car?" And he indicated another inebriated soul who was obviously *not* finding himself capable of remaining erect without support. As a matter of fact, he was preventing himself falling to the pavement only by hanging on grimly with both hands to my garden gate.

He did appear as if he might have some difficulty in making his way home at the present juncture on his own two feet. All the same, somehow I was not overwhelmed with enthusiasm by the prospect of conveying him homewards.

"I can see that he is much the worse for wear with too much drink," I said, "But why come to *me* to take him home?"

"Well," replied the other, "You're a minister and you have a motor car."

At that very moment two young men approached the garden gate, also on their way home from the public house and also having consumed some alcoholic beverages there but not, it would appear, to the same debilitating extent. Roman Catholics although they turned out to be, they were

quick to come to the assistance of the Protestant minister.

"What are you doing at the minister's door?" they shouted to the man standing before me. "Are you bothering him?"

"No, I'm just asking him to give my mate a run home in his car because he's not able to walk."

"You've a terrible nerve," they said to him. "Get your mate home yourself. We would never go near our priest with a request like that."

"Maybe not," was the rejoinder, as my caller moved back down the path to join them and his mate who was still embracing the gate, unable to let go. "But, you see, a minister's not a priest and a priest's not a minister."

From that beginning a vigorous discussion ensued about the Church and religion, with three of them going at it animatedly and the fourth blinking an owlish benediction on each of them in turn. After some ten minutes looking on and listening in, I shut the door quietly and returned to my chair. I do not think they ever missed me and some thirty minutes later I heard the voices quieten down a bit. I peeped out of the window to see the three of them join forces to prise the fourth's grip off the gate and proceed to shoulder him along the road.

Had I, through doing nothing, promoted some *ecumenical* activity?"

I must confess that, like most ministers, I have often let myself be 'conned' but I console myself with the thought that it is better to be taken in by a cheat than to refuse help to a genuine case of need. To the best of my knowledge I have never turned away a really deserving case. I hope not anyway.

chapter fourteen

some young people

I think, looking back, that probably the greatest volume of unspoiled pleasure that came to me in my ministry derived from the children with whom I had the privilege of working, especially the very young ones. At that age they are so trusting and so responsive, as well as being frequently disconcertingly frank, refreshingly naive or comically serious.

Our first grandchild, Martin Cole, was in High Carntyne Sunday School for a few years before the family moved to England. Therefore from the age of 2½ he sat with the beginners in the front seats of the church through the first part of Sunday morning worship, as our practice was.

He appeared to adjust quickly and easily to the fact of his grandfather occupying the pulpit and, although he used to give me intimate smiles and knowing looks from time to time, this was no great embarrassment to me, as a number of children were in the habit of offering me similar gestures of friendship. I discovered, however, after he had been attending Sunday School for some three months, that there was at least one thing about the matter that caused him some concern. One day he raised it with me, "Why," he asked me, "do people at the church call you Mr. Martin, when your name is 'grandpa'?"

This was a genuine puzzle to him at that age and it was a further reminder to me how important it is that we adults should try as hard as we can in our dealings with young children to look at things with their eyes and to think as best we can in their ways. We should also bear in mind—laying aside all false modesty—that some children, not just our own, are likely to hold us in great respect, amounting even to awe.

This is often one of the responsibilities a minister has to carry. At least one of our Sunday School youngsters thought I was God. After one Sunday morning service during which, in order to make a point in the children's address, I had descended from the pulpit, hoisted up my robes and run across the church, one child was heard to say to her mother in great excitement, "I saw God's legs today."

I always had a children's address as part of my morning service. Not every minister does; some think the children's address is an unhelpful interruption to the worship. They are, of course, entitled to their opinion and must conduct the church service as they think best. But I cannot agree with them. I believe strongly that it is good to have a part of regular Sunday morning worship where the children are specially in mind and where there is an opportunity to tell them something of the Good News.

Nor do I agree that laughter is out of place in the church service. I admit, without feeling any guilt or shame, that I often have tried to make the children laugh when I am speaking to them. This was not only because it was sometimes, as I saw it, the best way to illustrate the point I was making, but also because I want children to find the church a place they can enjoy being in.

Children's addresses took up a lot of my preparation time. It matters so much to get on the proper communication level alongside the children and that usually demands a lot of hard work. For nearly all of my 34 years in High Carntyne my children's addresses were built round the exploits of a fictitious five-year-old called Bobby. He became well known and apparently very well liked. After a few years it became more difficult to keep producing a fresh adventure Sunday after Sunday and I thought the time had come to let Bobby pass into oblivion—but there was a chorus of protest from his 'fan club', both young and not so young; and I had to keep him going, even though the effort required was sometimes very demanding.

On the day I retired from High Carntyne, six-year-old Kenneth Ross said to me, quite wistfully, "I'm going to miss you and I'm going to miss your stories about Bobby. Couldn't you put them in a book?" And that's exactly what I did! I treasure that comment and reckon that it alone recompenses me for all the sweat I lost over those stories.

I treasure, too, the memory of the marvellous little sketch entitled, "Ten Little Bobby Boys" which was the contribution of the Junior Section of the Boys' Brigade to a night the congregation staged to celebrate my semi-jubilee as their minister. It comforts and encourages me in face of the criticism I have encountered for my style of approach to the children in the Sunday service. And sometimes the criticism has been fierce.

During one television programme from High Carntyne I spoke to the children about following the leader (Jesus) and to try to make the point vivid I had them running round the church in pursuit of me. A very well-known senior minister of the Church of

Scotland was so upset by this that he had to write to the B.B.C. and express his outrage at the "sacreligious performance of a mountebank in church." I am happy to be able to say that his reaction was very much a minority one.

I liked the children to participate in the children's address, if not in physical activity such as in the follow-the-leader episode, certainly by way of giving answers to my questions. Mark you, I did not always elicit the answers I was hoping to get. One morning I was speaking about the Glasgow holiday period which had just begun.

"A great many people went away from Glasgow yesterday to Spain," I pronounced. "I wonder what takes them to Spain?"

Immediately a little hand shot up and five-year-old Grant Barclay called out, "*I* know—an aeroplane."

The answers and the comments of the children often took an unpredictable turn. But they all added to the happiness of the occasion and, I hope, also to the clarity of the particular message I was attempting to convey. Not infrequently, at any rate, they helped to keep my theological thinking fresh and relevant, as when, for instance, a youngster asked me, in genuine concern, "What keeps Jesus from falling out of heaven?"

My work with my older youth groups at Newarthill, at Newmilns and at High Carntyne also did a great deal towards keeping me up to scratch mentally and spiritually as well as providing me with a large measure of happiness and job satisfaction. I owe a large debt of gratitude to my Bible Classes and Youth Fellowships in the three churches I served—and not merely on account of the material benefits I owe to them.

These, however, were not inconsiderable. I suppose I may even have owed my life in a way to my Newarthill Bible Class. I was feeling rather seedy one Sunday and had a quite severe pain in my side. During the meeting of the Bible Class, it was noticed that I was somewhat under the weather and enquiries were made of me. When I mentioned the pain I felt, along with my other symptoms, a member of the class said, "I think you've got pleurisy. I've had it and that's exactly how I felt."

I discounted his diagnosis but I did not forget what he had said. That was why, when late that night the pain grew considerably worse, I allowed myself to be persuaded to let my mother send an emergency call to the doctor.

As the doctor came up the stairs to my bedroom I could hear him complaining to my mother about being called out late on a Sunday night for what was "probably something quite trivial." Once he had examined me his attitude changed completely. It was indeed a case of pleurisy and, he said, had we waited until the morning my situation might have been grave—and, had it not been for that boy in the Bible Class, we would undoubtedly have waited.

So it may well be that I owe my very life to my Newarthill Bible Class. On the other hand, when I came to think of it, I probably owed the pleurisy to it in the first place.

I had started up a Bible Class football team some time previously, and a good team it was, winning by far the most of its fixtures. I played at centre forward and enjoyed it immensely. A week previously I had been suffering from a heavy cold, when a match was due to be played, but no thought of calling off entered my head. As it happened, the match was played in a downpour and we had no bathing or showering facilities to follow the game. The following morning I woke up with the pain which later came to be diagnosed as pleurisy.

The material benefit I owe to my High Carntyne Youth Fellowship was of a different kind. It was entirely due to them that I made my first trip to the Holy Land. They expressed themselves as exceedingly grateful for the service I had rendered on their behalf and for the blessings they had gained through my ministry; and as a token of their appreciation they sent my wife and me on the Holy Land tour.

In a multitude of other ways—less tangible but also of treasured memory—I was indebted to my various youth groups. If I was of some help to them and I certainly hope that I may have been, they were undoubtedly of great help to me.

They also provided me with many memories of 'fun' times. The many Easter weekends I spent with my High Carntyne Youth Fellowship were a prolific source.

On one occasion we were joined late on the first evening by a member, George Dick, whose work had taken him out of the district for the past three months. During that period, unknown to him, one of our more senior members had got married and the recently married couple were also with us. George had a water pistol with him, and, when everyone had retired for the night, he decided to go on a good-natured rampage through the bedrooms, shooting water as he went. His rather juvenile escapade was terminated abruptly by himself as soon as ever he burst into the married couple's room. He came rushing to me, white of face, to exclaim in tones of shocked disbelief, "Charlie's up there in bed with a woman!"

The bus trips from Newmilns to the grand opera in Glasgow are highlighted in my memory, too—not least the very first of them. This was long before the days of Scottish opera but in those immediately post-war days Glasgow did have a regular opera diet provided by the annual season of the touring Carl Rosa Company. I was already an opera addict but had no car and public transport did not run late enough to make a visit to the opera possible by that means. It was, therefore, at least as much due to my desire to get to the opera as to my desire to introduce my Youth Fellowship to new horizons that I hired a 35 seater bus and booked 35 gallery seats for the Theatre Royal performance of La Traviata.

The Theatre seats—right at the top of the house—were 2/-each and I was able to offer my Youth Fellowship members the opera outing for 4/-a head. There was no lack of takers and in no time I had my required 35 names. But when we gathered at the bus on the theatre evening, I was amazed and appalled to see a girl joining the group who had given me neither her name nor her money, but who evidently thought she was one of the 35.

I could not, of course, send her home and so off we went. There were 36 of us in a 35 seater bus but that was little or no problem. What *was* a problem was the fact that we had only 35 theatre tickets for 36 would-be opera-goers. This circumstance produced what virtually amounted to a saga on its own.

In the bus I distributed the tickets to the 35 other passengers and reconciled myself to the necessity of purchasing a seat for myself at the box office with the possibility of not being able to get one close to my party.

The reality proved to be much worse. When I blithely presented myself (and my 2/-) at the box office I was informed that the gallery was sold out.

"But I must get into the gallery," I protested. "I have a group of 35 of my Youth Fellowship here with me and I must be beside them."

"I am sorry, sir," was the answer, polite but firm. "There simply is not a seat left."

"We could squeeze 3 into 2 seats or I could sit on the passage steps beside the others," I pleaded.

"I am sorry. That cannot be allowed. I am afraid there is no way you can gain admission to the gallery."

That door was obviously shut but I was not yet prepared to give up. I was determined to be with my group on this opera outing which I myself had planned and organised. And so I climbed up the stairs with them to the gallery—there seemed to be hundreds of steps leading up to the gallery of the Theatre Royal of those days.

"We have a group of 36," I explained to the usher at the door, "But, through a misunderstanding, we have only 35 seat tickets. Will you allow me to accompany them and squeeze in beside them somehow?"

As if he had not heard a word, he said to me, "Where is your ticket, sir?"

Patiently I repeated, "I do not have a ticket, that's the point, but it's important to be with my group. I am prepared to sit on the floor, if you like."

"You can't get in without a ticket. You must have a ticket."

"Can I stand at the back then? I could at least

see them at the interval and, of course, hear the opera as well if you let me do that."

"You must have a ticket. I can't let you in," were his final words as he washed his hands of me.

It was now very close to the time for the curtain to rise, and the inescapable fact was that we had only 35 tickets and 36 bodies. Knowing my passion for the opera, several offered me their ticket, but that was unthinkable. So they trooped into their seats while I scuttled back down the seemingly interminable stairs.

Back to the box office I went on what I was beginning to see was a pretty hopeless quest. Since the curtain was now up and the opera begun, the people in the box office had more time to listen to my tale of woe. They were sympathetic but insisted that they were unable to help. Even my renewed plea to be permitted to pay and stand at the back was rejected again.

"It's against the regulations. It simply can't be done."

"Well," I said, conceding defeat. "I'll just have to buy a ticket for another part of the house and join up with my group at the end."

"I'm sorry, there are no seats left anywhere. There *were* some earlier but they have all gone."

In desperation I said, "Could I see the manager? Perhaps he could be persuaded to stretch a point and let me in to stand somewhere since I am really in a spot."

Somewhat reluctantly the box office people agreed to this request, and directed me to the manager's office. I discovered him to be a charming man, and he listened to my tale with patience and with sympathy. It was nevertheless, he explained, utterly impossible for me to be admitted to the gallery. All the seats *were* sold and it was quite contrary to the very rigid regulations that I should either sit in the passageway or stand at the back.

"There is one thing I can do for you, however," he said. "We always keep one or two seats in hand for visitors and friends—not, I am afraid, in the gallery but in the more expensive region of the theatre. These are not all taken up tonight and I will be glad to let you have a seat in the grand circle with my compliments and you can rejoin your friends at the end."

By this stage I was relieved and delighted to accept his extremely kind offer. I had missed nearly all of the first act but I thoroughly enjoyed the rest of the performance, despite being on my own, and joined up with the others, without any further misadventures, for the journey home—and the wonderful fish suppers en route.

chapter fifteen

extra-parochial ministries

I have come almost to the end of my little book. There are many more 'tales of my ministry' that I would enjoy telling; but if you have read this far, you may well have had quite enough of them. I am going, nevertheless, before I close, to say a few words more.

Like every other minister I have found my ministry extending beyond what was actually done within the bounds of my own congregation and parish; and so I am going to make brief mention of what I might call my 'extra-parochial ministries', some of which have already received a passing mention in the pages of this book. In uniform or out of uniform a minister remains a minister wherever he or she may be and most ministers find themselves performing a number of extra-parochial tasks by virtue of their ministerial status.

But the first extra-parochial ministry of mine that I mention is a quite unofficial one. For a great many years I have been regarded as the unofficial chaplain of Motherwell Football Club, one of Scotland's premier league clubs. This position has never been by formal appointment. Rather, like Topsy, it 'just growed'; and I would not attempt to claim that my association with Motherwell F.C. was ever prompted by any sense of mission on my part. It was simply due to my passion for football.

While I was 'locum' at Newarthill, I was playing for Dalziel High School Former Pupils F.C. when we were drawn at home in the Scottish Amateur Cup against a team whose playing colours were similar to ours. This meant that we as the home team had to change our colours for the day. Since in those days we did not possess an alternative strip, I offered to try to borrow a set of jerseys from Motherwell F.C. whose manager was a member of the same church as I was, Mr. John Hunter, one of the game's truly great managers. He not only readily responded to my plea but also invited me to train at the Motherwell ground, Fir Park; and I have been doing that ever since, which now makes 46 years.

My association with professional football has been great fun for me, whatever good it may or may not have effected for anyone else; and I am grateful for the tremendous friendship offered me by a succession of managers and directors and many generations of players. I am grateful, too, for the multitude of interesting experiences it has given me. I will refer only to one of these—the wedding I conducted one day on the football field itself.

I received one morning a very polite letter from a young couple who told me that since they were both ardent Motherwell supporters, they had conceived the idea of being married on the playing pitch at Fir Park, if at all possible (during the close season, not in the middle of a match, thank goodness). They had, they told me, already approached the Board of Directors of the club who had readily granted permission for the wedding to take place on the pitch and had referred them to me as the 'unofficial chaplain' to see if I would be willing to conduct the ceremony. Their letter concluded by asking me most graciously if I would 'honour' them by doing just that.

I must confess to a lack of enthusiasm for 'gimmicky' weddings, but they were a likeable and sincere couple and, after meeting and talking to them, I agreed to conduct the marriage ceremony on the Fir Park turf. It was not without some misgivings that I went ahead. Indeed, the night beforehand I hardly slept through worrying about all the things that might go wrong and spoil the essentially religious part of the proceedings.

In the event it was a splendid and uplifting occasion for everyone present. The weather was brilliantly sunny and warm, Motherwell Football Club were excellently co-operative and helpful; and despite the batteries of press cameras in attendance and the presence of television crews in addition, we really did have a Christian marriage service. Ailsa Campbell and Ian Baillie were not only a handsome couple but an attentive and responsive one, and the congregation, accommodated in the grandstand, were equally so.

If I had had some anxiety before the event, I have had none since. I am very glad I took it on and have no doubt that, unusual though the setting was, I did the right thing in so doing. Even when the television news bulletins that evening introduced their coverage of the wedding with the theme tune for 'Match of the Day', the predictability of the cliché struck no discordant note—rather the reverse.

Most of my extra-parochial ministries, however, have been official appointments, such as my chaplaincy to Lightburn Hospital, for instance. I have to admit that I was in the beginning a most unwilling recruit to this branch of service. I had already declined

invitations to become chaplain to Barlinnie Prison, first of all, and then to Low Moss Prison. I felt I had more than enough to contend with in the large congregation and parish of High Carntyne. But when the Presbytery pressed me to accept the chaplaincy of the new Lightburn Hospital about to open not far outside my parish, I felt I could not give a third refusal.

I have never regretted my decision to accept this chaplaincy, reluctant though it was, and have greatly enjoyed the work involved. So much so that when I was retiring from High Carntyne and was of a mind to give up Lightburn also, since I was moving house fifteen miles away, I allowed myself to be persuaded to stay on; and I have never regretted that decision either.

A small hospital of 120 beds, plus a day hospital section, Lightburn has afforded me a lot of satisfaction, a good deal of fun and not a little inspiration. It is mainly a geriatric hospital with some stroke patients, too. Every Sunday afternoon since the hospital opened, we have held a short religious service in the hospital. These appear to have been a source of considerable help to many people over the years but not any more help, I am sure, than the Lightburn patients have given to me by the quite marvellous attitude many of them have shown to misfortune. This is typified by the way they love to sing the hymn, 'Count your blessings'. They would gladly sing it every Sunday, I believe, but although we do not quite do that, we sing it frequently and always with gusto.

> Count your blessings, name them one by one.
> Count your blessings, see what God has done.
> Count your blessings, name them one by one
> and it will surprise you what the Lord has done.

Over the 21 years of its existence and of my chaplaincy there, many Lightburn patients have counted their blessings in such a manner as has helped me to count mine.

Early in my time at High Carntyne I accepted an invitation, coming to me via my good friend, Professor William Barclay, to be industrial chaplain to William Collins Sons and Co., now Harper Collins. I have never felt that I was accomplishing very much in this capacity beyond simply flying the flag for the Church and the Gospel by making a regular weekly visit and by making myself available when required in any situation of need; but I have greatly enjoyed it. And this, too, has produced a rich crop of memories.

For instance, it could be said that the very first time I ever 'broadcast' a religious service was in the old Collins building in Glasgow's Cathedral Street. When I started as chaplain to Collins in 1957, Christmas Day was not yet a statutory holiday in Scotland and for most people was a working day. On Christmas Eve 1958 I held a short service in the canteen at midday but in 1959 I went in to the works on Christmas morning and conducted a brief act of Christmas worship over the public address system. I had no way of telling how this was going across—it was even much lonelier than I later discovered radio broadcasting can be, for on this occasion I was all by myself in a little room with a live microphone and neither engineer nor producer—although a surprisingly large number of people said kind things about it afterwards.

The exercise never needed to be repeated because in 1960 Christmas Day was a Sunday and by 1961, and ever since, Christmas has been a statutory holiday.

Whatever little help I may have given to Collinsians over these 32 years, my association with them has provided me with a lot of pleasure and not a little fun. I was not long begun as chaplain when an inter-department summer football league was started up. In those early days I had an office allocated to me in which I sat for an hour in the course of my weekly visit in order to be available for anyone who wished to see me about any matter. One day a young man, Hugh Gillies—who was to become a much loved Collins figure and whose early passing caused great sorrow—came to see me. Very diffidently he said, "I'm the secretary of the Litho Department football team and we know that you are a footballer(!). We would like you to play for us if you will but I must warn you that we are quite an old team. Some of them have even reached thirty years of age."

Considering that I was then thirty-seven, I was rather tickled but I was only too pleased to accept the invitation. This led to a lot of enjoyment and to a number of lasting friendships.

There were laughs, too, as in our first match. I had gone straight to the field from an official engagement and so was wearing my clerical garb. But Gordon Munro, who had not yet met me, did not see my 'uniform', as we were all stripped and ready for the fray before he arrived. Gordon, a likeable and warm-hearted fellow, was somewhat noted for his lurid language and I heard a bit of this during the game and in the dressing room afterwards—until I put on my clerical collar. Gordon went silent on the instant, the first and only time, his friends told me later, they had ever known Gordon rendered speechless.

I was also a school chaplain for practically all of my ministry. In Newmilns this meant no more than sharing in a church service at Christmas, Easter and the like; but in Glasgow it involved conducting a short weekly service, as well as participating in other school activities. I was chaplain first of all to Gartcraig Junior Secondary School which was exclusively for girls who had failed to reach a high enough examination standard to qualify for Senior Secondary. The policy of head teacher and staff here was based on the conviction that everyone, whatever might be her showing in examinations, had a talent; and it was their objective to discover each girl's best talent and to develop it. They did this marvellously well and, more than twenty years after Gartcraig ceased to be, I still encounter from time to time former pupils who speak with much affection of the school and what it did for them. The Gartcraig building may be long gone but many rich memories survive.

Gartcraig came to an end when the new comprehensive, Smithycroft Secondary, opened up; and I was invited to transfer my chaplaincy from one school to the other. Smithycroft, too, has given me a wealth of memories.

I treasure, for instance, the recollection of the young lad who managed to be outstanding among a large field of inveterate truants for the sheer consistency of his truancy. He scarcely ever came to school at all, except on a Thursday morning when he was rarely absent. On one of his frequent confrontations with him, the truancy officer focussed on this strange feature of his school attendance record.

"I notice that you are truanting from school practically all the time except on Thursday mornings and you are nearly always in school then. Why is that?"

"Well, you see," was the boy's reply, "Thursday morning is when the minister has his service."

Neither Robert Lamont, the then headmaster, nor I could ever work out what might have lain behind this Thursday morning addiction. Much as we would have liked to, we shied away from concluding that it was a case of the lad being 'gospel-greedy'—the rest of his record hardly justified that conclusion.

While that boy did not like to miss my school service, there was another whom wild horses would not have dragged to it, I fear. He belonged to a very exclusive Bible-based Christian sect and requested to be excused from attending the service on the grounds of conscience. Mr. Lamont said to him, "I would have expected you with your strong Christian commitment to want to attend what is a service of Christian worship. What is your objection to it?"

"It's because the chaplain speaks about the Bible during it," was the boy's reply.

What could be said to refute such a charge? Nothing, for it was true that I did speak about the Bible, albeit sometimes briefly. This, as I saw it, was what I had been called and commissioned to do. In everything I did as a minister, whether in the congregation or out of it, I tried to proclaim the Bible message of the Good News of Jesus Christ.

And that leads me, almost inevitably, to the theme of my closing chapter.

chapter sixteen

why did I choose
the ministry anyway?

Some readers may be wondering how I found my way into the ministry in the first place. They may well want to ask me, as indeed a number of people *have* asked me through the years, "Why did you choose the ministry anyway?"

The simple answer—over-simplified, no doubt, but nonetheless true—is that I did not choose the ministry. The ministry chose me or, rather, God chose me for the ministry. That was my belief at the beginning and it is my belief still.

I could, I think, have followed other careers and done so with some success and probable happiness. Other careers did for a time beckon me while I was still at school. I was quite a bright scholar and I think it was generally expected by those who knew me that I would 'do well' in life.

Around the age of fifteen, coming sixteen, I was in a bit of a dilemma as to whether to set my sights on school teaching or on medicine, both of which possibilities attracted me. Then I began to get disturbing feelings that pulled me in a totally different direction.

These feelings were strongest on Sunday mornings as I sat in church. Sunday by Sunday I seemed to hear a voice saying to me, as I looked at the minister in the pulpit, "Is that not a job you could be doing? Is that not the job you should be heading for?"

For many weeks I struggled against these promptings. To say that I did not relish the prospect of being a minister would be putting it mildly. The thought of it both depressed and frightened me. But it would not go away and it gave me little peace of mind. More and more it seemed to be insisting that this was God's call, God's command, to me. In the end I said to the inner voice that was refusing to be silenced, "All right, have it your way. I'll do it, I'll be a minister."

As soon as I made that decision I felt at peace and I knew then that it had truly been the voice of God and that I was answering his call. I have never doubted that this was so.

I have always remembered a comment made by my own minister when he learned of my decision to seek to enter the ministry. Somewhat wryly he said to me, "If you are going to be a minister, you must have three things—a genuine sense of vocation, a strong stomach and a thick skin." Well, my stomach could have been stronger and my skin was often proved much too thin; but my sense of call has never diminished.

I well remember also the comment made to me by a neighbouring minister at that time. "It's a very wise principle," he said, "that no-one should become a minister if he can possibly be something else." Even then, in my mid-teens, I fully understood what he meant; and now so many years later, I fully endorse it. Once I felt that God was summoning me to his work, there was little real choice left to me.

My family was disappointed when I told them I wanted to enter the ministry but were marvellously co-operative despite our very poor circumstances. My friends were puzzled, but tolerant. And I am grateful to God for calling me to this task. I can imagine nothing—despite all its frustrations and disappointments—that could provide the same job-satisfaction, nor anything that would have supplied me with anything like as much joy or as many blessings.

I remember with gladness many, many more people and many, many more incidents than I have set down in this book. I conclude with brief reference to other two.

On the Sunday morning that I announced to the congregation of High Carntyne that I had decided to retire at the end of the year, six-year-old Jane Simpson said to her mother, tearfully, at the close of the service, "That's the saddest news I've ever heard. He'll just have to change his mind."

The other instance also meant much to me at the time and means a great deal still. Like Jane Simpson's reaction and remarks, I take it to indicate a wealth of affection towards me, although it was expressed in a manner that might appear a little strange. Some two months before my retirement date was reached, I conducted the funeral service of one of my members. After the funeral, his widow said to me, "I am so glad that this happened while you were still our minister."

People and experiences of that nature are what make the Christian ministry so marvellously worthwhile.